I'VE GOT SOME LOVIN' TO DO

THE DORIS DIARIES ❖ VOLUME ONE

I'VE GOT SOME LOVIN' TO DO

THE DIARIES OF A ROARING TWENTIES TEEN

1925–1926

Edited by

Julia Park Tracey

iUniverse, Inc.
Bloomington

I've Got Some Lovin' to Do
The Diaries of a Roaring Twenties Teen, 1925–1926

iUniverse books may be ordered through booksellers or by contacting:

iUniverse
1663 Liberty Drive
Bloomington, IN 47403
www.iuniverse.com
1-800-Authors (1-800-288-4677)

Because of the dynamic nature of the Internet, any web addresses or links contained in this book may have changed since publication and may no longer be valid. The views expressed in this work are solely those of the author and do not necessarily reflect the views of the publisher, and the publisher hereby disclaims any responsibility for them.

Any people depicted in stock imagery provided by Thinkstock are models, and such images are being used for illustrative purposes only.

Certain stock imagery © Thinkstock.

ISBN: 978-1-4759-3984-2 (sc)
ISBN: 978-1-4759-3983-5 (hc)
ISBN: 978-1-4759-3982-8 (e)

Library of Congress Control Number: 2012913112

Printed in the United States of America

iUniverse rev. date: 07/31/2012

To all the Rebel Girls

All my life, my heart has yearned for a thing I cannot name.

—Andrée Breton

Contents

Gratitude

This work of heart was made possible by the loving support of my dear husband, Patrick Tracey, and my five children (Mia Romero, Simone Rodrigues, Savanna Tracey, Anastasia Rodrigues, and Austin Tracey). My mother, Elizabeth Bailey Park, and my aunt, Barbara Bailey Wellner, deserve kudos both for their assistance with this manuscript and for their patience and perseverance over the years. Thanks also to my father, William Park, for telling me to "go big."

Sister- and brother-writers who read, offered suggestions for, and supported this project include Dennis Evanosky, Mary Lee Shalvoy, Jordan Rosenfeld, Mhaire Fraser, Jack Mingo, and John Chilson; thanks also to readers Deanna Pervis, Kelly Conaboy Evans, Ginny Bauer Bucelli, Michael Singeman-Aste, Katje Sabin, Angela Barton, Emily Thayer, and Mary Ellen Morgan. Thank you to J. Astra Brinkman for amazing photographs. Thanks to Dennis Evanosky (again) and Eric Kos for photography, graphic design, and advertising support.

I also wish to give thanks to Lisa DeGrace of the Oregon Episcopal School for her own research into Doris's stay at St. Helen's Hall, and to the Oregon Historical Society and Oregon Public Broadcasting for their early support.

And thank you, Twitter and Facebook communities (my invisible friends), for your enthusiasm and generosity in helping me find my way around Portland (virtually speaking), identify defunct landmarks, and laugh all the way through the process.

Last, thank you to Great-Aunt Doris, who was kind enough to save her adolescent thoughts on paper and then in perpetuity, so that we could live them again.

Before the Diaries

"I never travel without my diary," Oscar Wilde famously wrote in *The Importance of Being Earnest*. "One should always have something sensational to read in the train." Doris Louise Bailey, the teenager who penned what we now call "The Doris Diaries," could have said the same.

The Doris Diaries are a lifetime's worth of diaries kept by Doris Bailey (later Doris Murphy), a Portland, Oregon, native who began keeping a daily record of her life as a fifteen-year-old in 1925. Doris Bailey Murphy was my great-aunt.

Doris Louise Bailey, age seventeen.

The diaries themselves are enchanting at first glance—filled with pen- and ink-scrawled daily gripes about school and stories of catching the streetcar and buying a new hat. But very soon, her use of contemporary slang (*pep, swell, gay,* and *sheik,* for example) and her daily occupations bring to life the rapidly changing world of the mid-1920s. New technology and social change abounded during this time: Young Doris talked on the telephone with boys, played tennis, and danced to records on the Victrola. Her parents, pillars of the white, Protestant, upper middle class of Portland, had been born and raised in Alabama in the post–Civil War era, with Victorian morals. But times were changing in the 1920s, and Doris constantly pushed the boundaries of what they thought was acceptable behavior for a young girl. She flirted with, kissed, and rode in cars with boys; she sneaked out the window at night, cut school, and chopped off her hair.

Her disdain for stolid conventions is evident in every entry. She was privileged, vain, judgmental, fickle, passionate, fashionable, consumerist, horny, untamed, and very romantic, imagining herself in and out of love with each passing day. And yet, she knew when her behavior was "not very nice," calling herself out, in effect, when she knew she'd pushed too far. In her room, at her desk, she soared into flights of fancy about the lonely souls living in the city she loved or an imagined idyll with her beloved Micky, and she wove a confusing tapestry of boyfriends (and a brother), seemingly all named Jack.

Doris cannot be removed from her context. She was writing in the mid-1920s, when it was commonplace to use racial slurs in casual conversation; indeed, she surely heard her father or brothers use such language. She did not hesitate to cross off her list of sweethearts boys who looked too "dago" or like "a Jew, boo hoo." In the 1920s, Portland, Oregon, was a bastion of the Ku Klux Klan. And it was simply unheard of for a girl in Doris's social position to befriend anyone outside of her race, class, and perhaps even religion (she attended the Episcopal Church). Doris also gave herself the freedom to swear in her diary (note her use of "d——," progressing to "damn," and the picturesque phrase "Son of a seacook!").

Doris's interest in politics and culture had not yet awakened in her teen years, as is evident by her attitudes and essentially shallow thoughts. But in later diaries (beginning in her college years in Portland and Arizona, 1930), readers see her sense of injustice against the oppressed (her transformation from oppressor to liberator) take root. She continued her growth from Portland debutante to a young social worker, literary publisher (of *The Dilettante*, a literary magazine, in 1934), and arts champion (e.g., Skidmore Arts Center, another pet project, in 1935) through the 1930s. Doris studied social work, shocking the Reed College community when she interviewed prostitutes in Portland for her thesis. The dean called her parents for a conference to discuss the scandalous behavior. She graduated from Reed in 1938.

Doris left Portland that year for San Francisco, where she worked with World War II refugees at the Red Cross and became active in the labor movements that were burgeoning across America. She flirted with joining the Communist Party and began an affair (not her first) with a married man. He eventually got a divorce from his wife, and Doris and Joe Murphy wed in 1948. They lived in San Francisco, where Joe was in labor leadership until the 1960s, at which time they retired to Occidental, California, a small town in the redwoods and vineyards of Sonoma County. Joe died in 1987.

The Aunt Doris I knew (great-aunt, actually) was blunt, interested to the point of intrusiveness, and impatient with fools. She was brusque when annoyed, but tender with those she loved. I knew her from my earliest years until her death in 2011; until the last month or so she was lucid and as feisty and unrepentant as ever. Her condom earrings are the stuff of legend. She rode horses into her seventies and saw clients in her private counseling practice into her nineties. She published her autobiography at age ninety-six.[1] From questioning me relentlessly about my boyfriends in my teen years to consoling me after a brutal divorce and always, always encouraging me and my daughters to aspire to artistic greatness, Doris was and remains a vivid presence in my life. I sit at her desk, a maple drop-front pigeonholed with cubbies for letters and notes. I eat from the dishes she used at her famous dinner parties. And on my right hand I wear a white sapphire and gold promise ring given to her by nobody knows whom. As much as I knew her, she remains a mystery.

---

[1] *Love and Labor*, by Doris Bailey Murphy.

Doris died at home, with her dog and cat nearby, at age 101 in March 2011. Upon her death, her trustee, my mother (daughter of Doris's brother Rae) discovered another surprise—the box of journals, kept so many years in a closet. As the writer in the family, I received these with joy and surprise, never having known of their existence. Discovering the historical settings and charming entries in these diaries has compelled me to seek publication for these gems of Americana—a glimpse at the twentieth century from a girl and then woman who would not be quiet and behave. A growing following on Facebook (www.facebook.com/thedorisdiaries) and Twitter (@TheDorisDiaries) further encouraged me toward publication of these diaries.

Although the life of one young woman may or may not have an impact on the historical context or the future of Portland, the daily views from a young person in 1925–1926 will certainly offer insight into local happenings and events, as well as cast light on cultural, societal, and technological changes, including early twentieth-century gender roles and feminist perspectives.

Historically, the Doris Diaries are a treasure trove of authentic American life in Portland in the mid-1920s. Doris cited people, places, and current events—popular culture such as Hollywood movies, new records, and new clothes and streets, buildings, and locations in Portland that offer a true sense of place. She noted the technologies such as automobiles, telephones, and elevators that also were transforming her city. She described in detail a school dance at the Hill Military Academy, boating fun at Lake Oswego, and a summer's adventure to a dude ranch in eastern Oregon, the O-O (Double O). Add descriptions of all these people and places through the eyes of an eager teen in 1920s vernacular, plus photographs of Doris and her friends and family, and you see before you the result of my endeavor.

Academically, the Doris Diaries are a primary resource for engaging with the early-twentieth-century feminist dialectic: Doris Bailey presents resistance to the rising patriarchy of the white privileged system and her perceived place in that society; the diaries illustrate one woman's tirade against collusion in her own oppression. "The relationship between feminism and the sexual revolution is central to understanding the broad social changes that affected U.S. society in the first decades of the twentieth century," one critic has suggested.[2]

Culturally, the diaries present a combination of *Bernice Bobs Her Hair*[3] and *The American Girls* stories. "Thoroughly modern"[4] Doris was a *real* American girl—and a definitive product of her age and era, awakening politically, sexually, and creatively.

My great-aunt Doris left a small bequest (smaller than she would have liked) to Reed College in her will. It is my hope that any financial gain from the diaries can go toward funding a scholarship at Reed for further feminist or historical study and, in this way, honor her legacy.

Note: I have kept her irregular or contemporary spellings, especially in words that have since changed, such as *goodby* and *down town*, and have kept her strikethroughs as well. Some words or names are unclear, and I have indicated that where necessary. Her spelling of proper names is sometimes inconsistent.

---

2 Leila J. Rupp, p. 289.

3 "Bernice Bobs Her Hair" (1920) is a short story by F. Scott Fitzgerald. It was made into a movie starring Shelley Duvall in 1976.

4 *Thoroughly Modern Millie* was a 1967 American musical film about the flapper era, starring Julie Andrews. It was taken to the Broadway stage in 2002, starring Sutton Foster.

The Baileys in Portland

Doris's father, Luther R. Bailey, was a respected architect in Portland. Born in Alabama in 1872, Bailey was raised in Hackneyville and attended Southern University in Alabama; he gave the valedictory address at graduation. He met Willie Doris Upshaw in Atlanta, and they married in 1901. Bailey later took his wife to Boston and graduated from Boston College with his master's degree in architecture. They had two of their five children there.

The Bailey family, June 1907, in Cambridge, Mass.: Luther R. Bailey, William Raeford (Rae), Willie Doris (Upshaw) Bailey, and Elizabeth Lee.

Bailey arrived in Portland in 1908. In 1910, he was the president of the Portland Realty and Construction Company. In 1911 he established a building contractor business under the name L. R. Bailey & Company and served as its president and manager. His World War I draft registration card lists his occupation as "architect" and his employer as "self." He worked from offices in the Northwestern Bank Building and was listed as an architect in the Portland city directories between 1912 and 1940.[5]

Bailey's designs and buildings included Colonial Revival, Prairie School, and Craftsman style homes. In addition to building his own houses on speculation, Bailey contracted with other real estate speculators, such as Edgar W. Smith, for whom he built most of the houses on an entire block between NE 19th and 20th Avenues and Siskiyou and Klickitat Streets.[6] Bailey designed and built the McAvinney Fourplex at 2004 NE 17th Avenue in Portland, which is on the National Register of Historic Places.[7] Other houses that Bailey designed and built include the 1911 Eugene Langdon House (2722 NE 22nd), the 1912 H. P. Palmer House (2410 NE 22nd), the 1912 George W. Hazen House (2106 NE 26th), the 1916 P. Schoniger House (3446 NE 19th), and the 1917 Edgar W. Smith House (2338 NE 20th). By the 1920s, Bailey had constructed some 100 houses in the Alameda and Rose City areas.[8] He designed buildings along Sandy Boulevard as well; family letters describe a movie theater and churches among them.

Willie Doris, born in 1878, was an Atlanta, Georgia, belle and daughter of a circuit-riding Baptist minister. Because of her slightly lower social status as a preacher's daughter, she was one of few young ladies at her college who did not have a "Negro" maid to assist her, according to family lore. She attended Judson College in Marion, Alabama, where she studied literature and history. Willie Doris was active in her church and community and served as the church hostess, in charge of luncheons and dinners (Doris often mentions serving at her mother's luncheons or her

---

[5] Kimberli Fitzgerald, p. 26.

[6] Note that in 1933 all the streets in Portland were given the N, NW, NE, SW, and SE identifier, and numeration on many of those streets also changed.

[7] Number 05001147 in the National Register database; the building was built in 1913 and listed in August 2005.

[8] Fitzgerald, ibid.

parents going out). Newspaper accounts of the weddings of Doris's friends indicate that Mrs. L. R. Bailey reigned over the tea and coffee service.

Willie Doris was a great reader and felt the lack of a library branch on the east side of the river. She was the motivating force in the establishment of the Rose City Park Library near 44th Avenue and Sandy Boulevard, according to family papers.[9] Willie Doris believed she was related to Robert E. Lee through her grandmother and was very proud of her Southern heritage. She was a charter member of the Robert E. Lee chapter of the United Daughters of the Confederacy and was active in that organization for many years. Her first daughter, Elizabeth Lee Bailey, was likely named for her esteemed distant cousin.

Doris's oldest sibling was William Raeford Bailey Jr. (my grandfather), who went by Rae, born in 1902. He later changed his name to L. Raeford Bailey like his father. Baby Elizabeth was born in 1906 and died in 1907; Willie Doris mourned the loss of Elizabeth the rest of her life. The death of this elder, unknown sister haunted Doris as well; she felt she could never replace Elizabeth or measure up.[10] Brother Joseph Albert Bailey was born in 1908 in Portland, and he and Doris were quite close; Joe is one of Doris's companions in many outings in this book. Doris was next, born in 1910 in Portland. Her youngest brother, Jack, baptized John Upshaw Bailey, was born in 1918 and was the baby of the family.

Luther Bailey and his family left Oregon in 1928 and moved to Arizona, but soon returned. Both he and Willie Doris died in Portland in 1948 and 1978, respectively.

---

[9] Upshaw Family Journal.
[10] See Doris Bailey Murphy's autobiography, *Love and Labor,* for Doris's feelings about her late sister.

1925

June 12 to Feb 18 1926
Love is Life
UNIVERSITY
LOOSE LEAF
NOTE BOOK
No. H-803
NAME
ADDRESS
Portland Oregon
Diary
EXTRA FILLERS NO. H-803-F CAN BE
OBTAINED AT WOOLWORTH STORES

Sunday, July 12[11]

I have decided to keep a diary in which I can confide my dreams, my hopes and ambitions. I went to C.E.[12] today. There was a Christian Endeavor delegate from Los Angeles there. He gave a perfectly marvelous talk. He was only about 18 and *so* good looking. I used to say that religious boys were silly things, but I've changed my mind. This boy has done more to influence my life than all of Daddy's lectures can begin to. I see things in an all together different light than I did before. This boy is just the type I am going to marry. I'm through with all this silliness. Boys kissing you good night and etc cetera [*sic*]. It's the bunk, and starting tomorrow, I'm going to lead a straightforward spiritual life.

Monday, July 13

Hot day. I tried to think uplifting thoughts, but (I must be truthful) ice cold lemonade and a book appealed to me more.

Tuesday, July 14

Lily[13] and me went to the park tonight. We were swinging and asked a boy to swing us. Then we decided to come home. The darn fool then followed us all around. He was dago looking[14] and rather nice in his speech but so greasy and awful. He repelled me. It was practically impossible to get rid of him. And finally we had to take the bus. Even then I think he would have come with us, but I said goodby and gave him a broad hint to beat it. I *hate* boys. They're such vulgar creatures.

---

11 At the time of this entry, Doris is fifteen years old.

12 Christian Endeavor (C.E.) was a Christian youth organization; it was influential in supporting the temperance movement in the 1920s.

13 The Baileys' maid. (Doris's mother hadn't had a maid at college, but the Luther Bailey family had one or more servants.)

14 Doris uses derogatory slang for an Italian or Hispanic person.

Wednesday, July 15

Oh Gee! But I'm happy. How can I describe it? Marjie[15] came over and said she had something *wonderful* to tell me. I took it nonchallany [*sic*; nonchalantly] at first because of course I didn't think it was anything important. She's always raving about somebody. This is what she said. She went down town yesterday and Jack *Freidel* sat beside her. He asked her if she wasn't the girl that chummed around with that tall blond with the marcelled[16] hair. She said "yes," and he wanted to know my name, address and et cetera. Just imagine it. He actually NOTICED me. He said, "Don't you think she has pretty eyes?" Oh, I'm excited. And all this time I thought he didn't even know or care I was on the map. Oh! Oh! Oh! I wish I could talk to him. He even wanted to know what street car I took down town. Oh Joy, Joy, Joy. Dear Diary, you can't understand how I feel about him.

Mary Lois Dana, known as Marjie, was Doris's best friend; she is seventeen in this photo.

15 Mary Lois Dana, "Marjie," was Doris's best friend.
16 A short, wavy hairstyle. The Marcel Wave (sometimes spelled "Marcelle") was a stylish wave given to the hair with heated curling irons.

Friday, July 17

I couldn't resist the temptation to call Jack F. up today. He knows who I am and said he was going to call me Billy Bailey.[17] Oh, he was so nice, I almost loved him. I was ashamed for calling him up, so I told him that a girl bet me I wouldn't like him if I knew him. I was trying to get acquainted with him. He believed me and said that he would help me win the bet.

Tonight I wanted to go for a walk with Marjie. I had a heck of a time getting out. Daddy said I had to be in by 8:30. Wouldn't that make a person mad? Anyway, we went and got a "Sunday,"[18] then walked down to school. Before we realized it, it was 9 o'clock. I decided I'd have to take the bus. I was standing watching for it. When I did see it, my heart jumped in my mouth. Jack F. was on it *with another girl*. And *his arm was around her.* Of course I didn't take it. I pretended that I was just crossing the street. When he saw me, he barely recognized me. Oh, death, where is thy sting? Why can't boys turn out to be what you think they will? I'm off of boys from now on. They're just a fickle, conceited sex that aren't worth looking at. And I shall put Jack F. out of my life. Close the doors of my heart and forget that he was ever alive.

Saturday, July 18

I went down town today. When I got home, Lily said that Jack F. had called up. She had talked to him, letting him think it was me. He said, "Why didn't you get on the bus last night?" and she said, "Because you were on it." He said, "I thought that was it." Then she let him know he wasn't talking to me. He laughed and asked her a lot of questions about me that she answered. Of course, I didn't get on the bus because he was on with another girl, but I didn't want *him* to know it. Lily told me all this and I was so mad I phoned him up and said, "Jack, I've just found out that someone has been playing double. Possibly she told you lots of things that

---

17 From the popular 1902 song "Won't You Come Home, Bill Bailey," words and music by Hughie Cannon.
18 Ice cream sundae.

aren't true, among them, that I didn't get on the bus because you were on it. I want you to know that you don't influence my life that much."

Then he said, "Well, why did you run a block to catch it after I got off, then?" I was stumped then and didn't know what to say. Somehow I changed the subject, and I said, "Besides, you seemed pretty absorbed in the girl you were with. It's a miracle you even saw me."

"The girl I was with?" he gasped, and then began to laugh and laugh. That made me mad, and I was just about to hang up when he said, "So that's why you didn't get on. Why, that was my mother." Of course, I was terribly relieved but I didn't let him know it. I was mad that I had let him know that I had even noticed him, so I said coldly, "Well, goodby, Jack—oh, I lost the bet." And hung up. I guess I'll never see or hear from him again.

[scrawled across top of page] I hate boys

Thursday, July 23
I haven't written for a long time because there hasn't been anything to write. Jack F. called me up today. He didn't say much. Will came to see Joe [Doris's brother]. Hot week. Dull life.

Wednesday, August 5
Gee, it's been long since I've written. I came out to Marjie's[19] today. There's a boy named Ned that she likes. I met one named Fridze. He's cute as the dickens. I want to get well acquainted with him. And I'm going to tomorrow, by heck.

---

[19] The Danas lived at Oak Grove—outer district of Portland on the Willamette River.

Thursday, August 6

Oh boy, I'm happy, happy, happy. We went swimming today. As I said before, I [was] determined to get well acquainted with Fridze. At first he didn't pay me much attention. Then he pushed me off the float. Of course, that broke the ice between us, and our acquaintance had begun. Then things began to get pretty dull, so I procured a blanket from Ed and lay down beneath one of the canoes, presumably to sleep. The boys turned another canoe in front of this one, which made me a regular little room. Then they began to pester me, and although I pretended I was angry, it was fun. I heard a commotion at the end of the canoes but pretended I was asleep. After the commotion had subsided, I heard a snicker and opened my eyes. My heart stood still. Fridze had crawled in and was lying beside me. His gray eyes bent upon me. For a while we just looked in each other's eyes. Then one of the boys yelled, "Come on, Fridze, we've got to hit for home."

Fridze said, "Uh-uh. I don't wanta."

Then the boys laughed and said, "I don't blame you, old kid."

Fridze said to me, "Hear that? It's a compliment."

I did hear it all right and made Fridze get out. There's no telling what the others would say, and I'll admit, it didn't look very nice. We swam around after that, and when it was time to go, he offered to buy me a hot dog.

Friday, August 7

We went swimming again today. Frankie (a boy I hate) pushed me off the float, and I said, "Just for that, you have to let me use your canoe." I ran and got in it, and he said, "I will, if you'll let me go with you." And I let him. We went way up by the bridge, and he was *so* nice. On the way back I said, "Gee, I'm having such a good time, and to think I have to leave it all."

He said, "Why?"

And I said, "I'm going home tomorrow."

"What!" he said, and commenced to make the biggest fuss. I can't remember everything he said, but it was awfully flattering. I got all puffed up. He wanted my address, telephone number, and everything. That evening after Marjie and me got home, he called up and wanted to know if he could come over. We sat out on the bluff underneath the stars. Oh boy, but it was romantic. Of course he attempted to kiss me when he left, but for some reason I didn't let him. I wish I had now. I'm blue.

Teens swimming at The Oaks, including Rae (center).

Saturday, August 8

I went home this morning and had just gotten home when Marjie phoned, and I came out again. While I was home, Mother said Jack Freidel called me up. Oh boy! We went swimming today, and Fridze wasn't there. Maybe, just maybe, he didn't come because he knew I wasn't [supposed to be there]. I had fun, though. Ned (Marjie's beau) is beginning to pay me lots of attention.

Sunday, August 9
Went swimming again, and Fridze wasn't there. I asked Ed where he was, and he said in Oregon City. Jack Waldron was there. The boy I met at the dance. He was nice to me.

Monday, August 10
Fridze was at the beach today. He went home early *with another girl*. I don't care, tho. I had lots of fun. Glen seems to like me. Took me for a canoe ride. In fact, all the boys were exceptionally nice to me. For some unknown reason.

Tuesday, August 11
We went down to the beach in our clothes today and took our suits. The boys paid me so much attention. Especially Fridze. I don't understand it, but I paid him back for yesterday and went for a ride with Ed. That reminds me. Ed said he was going to make me swim the river, so with the help of three other boys, he tied me up, put me in a boat, and took me across the river. Then he dumped me out. There was nothing I could do but swim, so I swam. I got awfully tired, but he wouldn't let me in the boat.

I *hate* Frankie.

Wednesday, August 12
Nothing unusual happened today.

Thursday, August 13
Cloudy day, didn't go swimming.

Friday, August 14
It was still cloudy today, so Marjie and I dressed up in hiking clothes and went over to explore the old mill where there was a rumor that the convicts were hiding. This was exciting while it lasted, but it didn't last long. We went back to the float, and the boys dared us to walk out on the log. We took up their dare, and when we were out in the middle of it, the boys started rolling it. Of course we fell off, and it was the awfullest sensation you can imagine. I felt like a ton of lead, and when I looked to shore for sympathy, I saw only a crowd of boys so convulsed with laughter, they were holding their sides. When I crawled up out of the water, they burst out afresh and said, "You look so fun-nn-y." Of course this didn't make me feel any better, so I calmly asked for a mirror. There, my worst fears were realized, and I said, "I'm disgraced. I'll have to hide." I ran around the boat house, and they caught me. Then the boys calmed down and built a fire.

Saturday, August 15
Jack W. was there today. I think he likes me. Fridze, too, for that matter.

I think Jack W. likes me. At least he says so!!?!

Sunday, August 16
Had lots of fun today. Ned took me for a canoe ride. Oh boy but Marjie was jealous. Jack W. took my [purse?] home with him and brought it over tonight. Ned came with him. I have high hopes of success.

~~I think he really likes me.~~

Monday, August 17
Fridze is quite slavish. In fact, I'm beginning to tire of him. I wish his hair wasn't so long.

Tuesday, August 18

The boys made quite an event of my going away. Fridze kissed me goodby behind the boat house. Not so bad at that. Ed said, "Are you going to kiss me goodby, Doris?" Right before everybody. I felt so funny. I made up with Frankie because—as I told him—"I hate to have an enemy behind me. They're dangerous."

I took the boys' pictures, and they seemed to like it. When it finally came time to leave, there was a lump in my throat. It's strange how attached one can become to a bunch like that. Mr. Mead took us up in the launch. I looked back and waved to the boys till we turned a bend in the river and I couldn't see them.

Wednesday, August 19

Came home today. Gee, it was good to see Marg S. I went to the show with her and saw Jack G. Even he was good to see. Even though I had fun at Oak Grove, "Be it ever so humble, there's no place like home."

Thursday, August 20

I saw Lloyd and Perry today. Gee, it was good to see 'em.

Friday, August 21

Took Marg S. up to the new house.[20] I guess she likes it pretty well. We move Tuesday.

---

[20] The Baileys moved from the house at 1320 Alameda Avenue to 274 Culpepper Terrace, both in Portland. Doris's father designed and built both houses. The streets were not given the N, NW, NE, SW, and SE identifier until 1933, so neither Alameda Avenue nor Culpepper Terrace had that designation at the time of this diary.

Saturday, August 22
Nothing unusual. Dull life.

Sunday, August 23
Went to C.E. with Marg S. She's falling for Hal. Oh well, who wouldn't fall for those baby blue eyes of his. I did once myself. But thank goodness I got over it. The boy I mentioned on the first page of my diary was there also. I had forgotten all about my good resolutions. Oh well. You're only young once. Why not make the best of it and have a good time. There's plenty of time to be serious when I'm middle aged.

Monday, August 24
I stayed all night at Margie's [not Marjie Dana's]. About 12 [midnight] we went for a walk around the block. We heard some music in one of the houses and crept up to listen. We soon discovered that a booze party was being staged. We listened for about 45 minutes and some of the things they said! Oh *boy*.

Tuesday, August 25
We moved today. I'm writing at my new desk. I'm *crazy* about my furniture.

**The Bailey children had desks in their bedrooms.
This one is Rae's, circa 1918.**

Wednesday, August 26

Alyce and Marjie came over this afternoon. I'm afraid Alyce's vacation in this hick town she went to didn't do her any good. She's worse off than she ever was. Poor kid. She's only 13, and she knows more than I do right now. A girl 16 would hardly talk—oh well, I'll be picking her to pieces in a minute.

Thursday, August 27

Nothing unusual except I arranged to meet Marge at the circus and missed her, so I spent my circus money for stationery. I'm beginning to fear nothing exciting will ever happen again. When I look back at the eventful days at [the] Danas' and then compare them with this week, I feel like weeping. Not even a boy to flirt with. I wonder what girls Fridze and Frankie and Ned and Johnny are rushing. I saw Charley Pringle down town today. He's rather cute.

Friday, August 28

Went down town again for lack of any other excitement. Saw Art Young, and he walked from the entrance of Meier & Frank's[21] to the fifth floor with me. I was flattered, I'll admit. When I told him I wasn't going to Grant [High School],[22] he said, "*Gee*, Doris, that *is* too bad. We'll miss you terribly." Um. Not so bad at that, is it, old top. Congratulations!

Meier & Frank was the premier department store in downtown Portland.

---

[21] Meier & Frank department store, established 1857. It was later purchased by May Company and then became Macy's.
[22] Grant was a new high school, opened in September 1924. Lincoln had opened in 1869 as Portland High; it was renamed Lincoln High School in 1909 during the "Lincolnmania" surrounding the 100th anniversary of Abraham Lincoln's birth. The building where Doris attended class was built in 1912.

Saturday, August 29

Mr. Dixon and Mrs. Van de Carr were here from California today. Mrs. Van de Carr brought me the loveliest purse. It cost seven dollars. Um. Mr. Dixon had his son with him who is 19. He stayed to dinner also. He was very good looking and had a very strange personality. He was awfully nice to me. After dinner we sat on the porch a while and then danced. He said I danced like a little feather. I think I made a big hit with his father, too. He made a big fuss over me anyway. I like Mr. Dixon. He's an Englishman and very eccentric. He is so well bred without being the least bit stiff or over-formal. They say he is worth lots of money. He used to be a banker but is retired now. The son has a car of his own.

Speaking of money, Mrs. Van de Carr said she left me $2,000 worth of jewelry in her will. Um. Better and better.

[across top of page] *I don't care. I* do like *Jack.*

Sunday, August 30

Went to C.E. today. That boy was there, and I found out his name was Ciril. He's twenty years old and in his second year of college. He doesn't look a day over seventeen. I think he's crazy about Lucy, tho. So I haven't much chance, I'm afraid. Lloyd came over this afternoon. He's a pretty good old scout. I had on a pretty suit today. I'm sick of boys, tho. I think I'll swear off of them.

Say, Alyce and me did a silly thing this afternoon. Nobody else but us would do it. We went to Christian Endeavor and got there about a half hour early. We decided to go for a walk. We passed a pretty house, and Alyce said, "I wonder what the house looks like inside. Let's go ask if Sally Smith lives there, and then we can see the inside of it." I said, "Shall we?" And she said, "Of course not, silly." But [in] some way it appealed to me, so I said, "If you'll go ask at that small house across the street, I'll ask here," which was a perfectly foolish thing to do, but we wanted excitement.

Alyce asked at the small house, and then I took a big breath, and we went to the big one. I said, "Does Sally Smith live here?"

"Why, no, she doesn't."

"Oh, I see. Thank you, we were told she lived on this street in a stucco house, but I guess it's farther down."

"Well, you see," he answered, "I'm pretty well acquainted with all the stucco houses along here, and this is the only one on this street."

I was getting pretty panicky, especially since he was good looking, so I said, "This is 42nd, isn't it?" I knew it wasn't.

"No, this is 44th," he answered. "But I'm sure there is nobody by the name of Smith on 42nd. Ah, has she a phone?"

I fell into the trap. "Yes."

"Well, perhaps you would like to look her up in the phone book."

Oh, hell, what could we do? I looked at Alyce, and she returned my stare. Why couldn't she help me out? I wanted the earth to open and swallow me. Then an idea came to me. "She lives with her aunt," I boldly stated. "And we don't know her aunt's name. You see, the fact of the matter is that we hardly know her. I'll admit we're terribly indefinite and ill-prepared to look anyone up. I'm awfully sorry to have troubled you. I guess we'll have to give the matter up." And I pulled Alyce down the steps. We were almost down when he said, "Oh, girls, maybe it is the other side of Sandy [Boulevard]." I said, "Yes, I remember, that's it." And [we] walked down those stairs so fast I'm afraid it was noticeable.

Tuesday, September 1

Oh boy—Jack called me up tonight. Oh, I like him, I do, I do, I do. His voice was so manly and strong. Oh, I would that I could see him. To be near him, oh, oh, oh. He's WONDERFUL. Marjie don't like him, but I don't care. In fact, I'm glad she don't. I hate competition. Oh how I like him. If I were older and he was older and I got to see him more, I *know* I could love him with all my heart and sole [*sic*]. Oh, Jack, Jack, Jack!!!

Wednesday, September 2

Nothing unusual today. Awfully hot.

Thursday, September 3

The folks went out tonight, so I went to bed early. I had just dozed off to sleep when the phone rang. I answered it with a gruff, "Well?" and Jack F.'s cheery voice came singing across the line. I was never so happy in all my life. We gossiped a while. Talked about the wreck of the *Shenandoah*,[23] and Lincoln and Grant [high schools]. He told me that Mr. Warfield was married, and we gossiped a while about him.

It was lots of fun. Then he wanted to know when he could see me and when I was coming over to Marjie's, and if I was, was I going to stay all night, and oh, just everything. I'm so happy. And who wouldn't be? *Gosh.* He wanted to know what school I was going to and, oh, everything. Oh, oh, oh.

---

23 The USS *Shenandoah* was a rigid airship and made the first crossing of North America by airship. On September 3, 1925 (same date as the diary entry), on its fifty-seventh flight, *Shenandoah* was torn apart in a squall over Ohio.

[across top of page] *Oh Jack Freidel Go To Hell*

Friday, September 4

Alyce and I went out to Oak Grove, saw Fridze. None of the other kids, tho. It was such a disagreeable day, but we had fun anyway. I am staying all night at Alyce's.

Saturday, September 5

Nothing unusual. Got me a new sport hat. Mother will probably kick a fuss, but I can't help it. I don't want to go to Lincoln [High School]. I know they can't possibly fathom how bad I [don't] want to go, or they couldn't, they wouldn't send me there. I WANT TO GO TO GRANT.

Sunday, September 6

I don't think I've ever spent such a dull day in all my life. School starts Tuesday. Bah! Anyway, it will relieve the monotony. If I was only going to Grant. Oh, I want to go so bad. Mother managed to restrain her joy when I showed her the hat. I'm hoping to get a new coat sometime next week.

Jack's picture is sitting in front of me on the desk. It's enough to inspire me into a burst of sentimental poetry if I wasn't so dog-on [*sic*] sleepy.

Monday, September 7

Another dull day. I don't want to go to school. *Damn.* I went for a ride in Evan's Buick Roadster today.

A thunderstorm is raging outside. I won't admit it, but I am scared, just a little. I wish Jack would call me up.

Tuesday, September 8

Oh, I *hate* school. *I do, I do, I do.* The girls are all so snobby and everything. I went over to Grant to get my transfer slip. It made me so homesick to be there where I knew everybody. I wanted to cry, and I did, by heck.

Marjie went to get her hair cut today. She had it cut in a boyish bob and looked so adorable that I had mine done. I look perfectly hideous. Rae [Doris's brother] said that he wouldn't be seen on the street with me and that I looked cheap and everything else mean that he could think of. Oh, I'm perfectly miserable, and I've got to go to school tomorrow and stand the gaze of millions. Oh, oh, oh. Death, where is thy sting?

Tuesday, September 15 (or thereabouts)

I haven't written for so long because I have been so busy at school. I get so homesick for Grant and the girls at times that I can hardly stand it. Lincoln don't compare with the good old blue and gray.

Jack called me up tonight and did his best to make me feel all the more homesick by telling me all about how the lawn had grown and who was President of the Student Body and a lot of other small things that serve in the [illegible] of a school. He was nice, tho, said he wished I was at Grant and everything. Then Daddy made me quit talking to him, and I'd only talked ten minutes. *Mean,* that's what I call it.

Wednesday, September 16

Oh, the *cutest* boy sits across from me in English. He has black curly hair, and when he studies, he runs his hand through it so that little curls fall down on his forehead and make him look adorable. He has dark smooth skin and the most wonderful blue eyes. They are such a contrast to his black hair. But when he smiles!—OH! Words fail me. He was so sober today, and then someone said something funny. He looked across at me and laughed. His face was transformed. I caught my breath, I was so fascinated. I've never in all my life seen anything to equal that WONDERFUL smile of his. Honestly, if I were him, I'd smile all the time.

Oh, I *like* him.

He wears a gray suit.

I can't hardly wait till tomorrow.

Thursday, September 17
Oh, he was so *nice* to me today. It's the first time he has showed any interest whatsoever in poor little me. And he *kept* talking to me.

Friday, September 18
Oh, sweet bliss, I'm lucky. He wanted to know my reg. room [home room] today, what course [schedule] I was taking. And everything. Several times when I should happen to glance at him, he would be sitting there just regarding me so intently. Oh, it would be thrilling. When the period was over, he took my paper up to the desk. Of course I went out the door, and he caught up with me and walked down the hall with me. Think of it. Gee, I'm happy. He's so good looking, and to think he would walk with me. Oh. I saw him seventh period in the hall, and he smiled so nice and said hello so sweetly. He has the most wonderful smile I ever hope to see. His eyes kind of close, and little lines go out at the sides. Oh, I can't explain it, but his whole face smiles instead of just his mouth. And when he smiles at me, I'm in heaven *absolutely.* My head just goes soaring above the clouds, and I can think of nothing else. And oh, I've got to wait clear til Monday. DARN THE LUCK.

I wonder why Jack didn't call up. By the way, this boy is lots better looking than Jack.

Saturday, September 19

I came out to Marjie's today. Went to a show.

Sunday, September 20

Went to Sunday School and saw Jack Waldron.

Monday, September 21

He was kind of indifferent today. I can't imagine why.

Tuesday, September 22

Oh, I'm happy, happy, so happy. Everything has been wonderful today, and I'll start from the beginning. In English this morning, Micky was just wonderful. I showed him a poem I had written, and he said that I looked like I ought to be a poet or artist. Then he walked down the hall with me again. Oh, he was simply divine. Then about seventh period I told the Dean I was sick, and she excused me for the rest of the day. I went over to Grant and got there just as school was letting out. Oh, it was so good to see everybody. Even Jack Pillar. Then Marjie, Alyce, and I went over in the gym to watch the boys play foot ball. They were outside and we were looking from the windows. Then my heart gave a leap. I saw Jack Freidel. He passed under our window and looked at me kind of funny.

Then he passed into the gym. We girls didn't want to be caught in there on a boys' gym day, so we beat it. I went lingeringly because he was so good looking. I fell in love with him all over again. Then tonight he called up. He wanted to know why I ran away. He said that after he got dressed, he went upstairs in the gym and went over to the building and everywhere looking for me. Just imagine, isn't that wonderful?

I said, "Then you know who Marjie and Alyce are, don't you?" He said, "No. I only noticed you. I didn't even see them. I couldn't take my eyes off you." Then he wanted to know when I was coming again and to be sure and let him know, and oh, I love him so.

Wednesday, September 23

Micky walked down the hall with me again today. He's awfully cute, but I wish he would comb his hair. I liked it at first, for a change. But now I'd like to see it the other way. I think he would look cuter.

I can't keep from thinking of Jack today. I'd give my new coat right now if I could be at Grant instead of Lincoln. Oh, Jack, Jack, Jack. Micky is awfully cute but—oh, I don't know. I'm hungry for Jack. My own, my beloved, come to me. I feel so romantic tonight. I want love, romance, laughter, romance, thrills, and so forth. I have a feeling tomorrow is going to bring forth something unusual. I hope so, all right.

Thursday, September 24

Micky is awfully nice. I showed him a poem Marjie had written. He wrote a note and said, "Gee, you're *great*, but you ought to be a reformer or something." Of course I hadn't meant him to think it was me. But it made such a hit with him that I lived the lie. I think I would have told him if—oh, if—he hadn't put it in his pocket NEXT TO HIS HEART. Of course that was the last straw. I want him to think I'm clever, and so I guess this is my only chance. Tho it's an awful thing to do. I wonder if Marjie will ever forgive me. I love her so, but I like him awfully well, too. I'm going to call her up the first chance I get and tell her. Oh, I like him so.

Oh, say, I was walking around the block with Margret today at noon, and one boy said, "Didn't I see you at Atlantic City[24] this summer?" I said, "No, why?" And he said, "Weren't you in the beauty contest?" Um!

---

[24] The Miss America contest began in Atlantic City, New Jersey, in 1921. Beauty contests were all the rage.

Friday, September 25

Micky was indifferent today for some reason. But oh, just wait. There is a boy that lives only three doors from here. I've seen him several times at Lincoln. He was awfully cute, wore golf knickers, and dressed just spiffy. But he looked like he would be "stuck up." However, Joe [Doris's brother] got acquainted with him and liked him. He also informed me that he had invited him up for tonight. (Mother and Dad were going out.) So I phoned Marjie D. and asked her to come up and spend the night with me. She did. After I was introduced to him, we danced. He is a wonderful dancer. Then we made candy. About that time we were getting real chummy.

And then someone suggested that we tell ghost stories. We turned off every light and sat on the couch. He put his arm around me and oh, I got a thrill. Well, that was the beginning. He got nicer and nicer, tho he seemed to like Marjie awfully well. I don't blame him for that, but I'm getting off my track. We were all sitting there peacefully when all of a sudden Rae turned the lights on. We all jumped up on one accord. Rae just laughed and went on out. Gene said that we might as well go where we wouldn't be interrupted. So we went for a walk. We walked way up to the top of the terraces and stood looking down on the lights of Portland. I was never so enthralled in all my life. It was as if we were standing on the top of the world, looking down on the lights of civilization. Down there was glamour, life, gaiety, man-made things. Above was Nature's work. All was so still where we were. Just the stars, the woods, the moon, and us. I think we were all affected the same. For a moment before, Gene had been talking and laughing. Now he was still, and his face had taken on a beauty indescribable. And it was breathtaking. It was all so big and majestic. We were away from the petty, trivial things that make the modern life and were out in the great open spaces.

Then I began to think of how small we four were on the face of the earth. Just like flies. Just products of humanity that come and go as do the seasons. I must have shivered at the awe of it, for he put a protecting arm around me, and we turned to go. Neither of us said a word for a long time. We could not, it seemed, break the spell or trance that hung over all.

**The view from Culpepper Terrace at the time the
Bailey home was built or under construction.**

Then he had to go and spoil it. We passed under an ark [*sic*] light, and he said, "Look, Joe. I bet you wouldn't have the nerve to do this in the light." And he took me in his arms and kissed me. Of course it was thrilling, but I wasn't in the mood for that just then. I had hoped he was thinking of the spiritual, worthwhile things of life. And then I thought, maybe he couldn't break the trance and was so enthralled that he had to kiss me. He did it so tenderly and gracefully.

Oh hell!

~~Then he said, "I know how you feel, but I couldn't shake the spell any other way, so please, don't seem so preoccupied. I thought a kiss would awaken you from your trance, but I see it only lengthened it. Please try to forget it and I will, too. I appreciate your love of beauty, but tonight, let's have gaiety." He was so appealing that I consented. So the rest of the walk was~~

~~spent in laughter and jokes.~~ I like him [illegible] awfully well, although I'm still true to Jack F., and I don't know about Micky.

Saturday, September 26

I couldn't keep my mind off of Gene today. I acted like such a fool last night. Just think, to know a boy only two or three hours and then let him kiss you. It's awful. I hate myself for a sentimental idiot.

I was thinking today of the six boys I have ever been interested in and compared them today. First was Perry, red hair, conceited, polished idiot. I want to forget him, so I think I'll say five boys. It's nicer. There is first Jack Freidel with his strong vivid character towering above them all, fine stately carriage, black straight hair, keen piercing gray eyes, and strong, purposeful chin.

Then: Jack Pillar. Short, well built, athletic, mop of brownish-black curly hair, brown eyes, serious. By no means a sentimental fool.

Then: Fridze. I always have a picture of a laughing, jolly boy. Black hair and big, frank, boyish laughing gray eyes. Rather weak character but full of fun and laughter. Always on the go. Never bothering to be serious.

Then Micky. Medium height, brown hair, blue eyes, all very common looking until he laughs, and his smile is his fortune, so to speak. A chin full of character, serious except at odd moments when he laughs a happy, breathtaking laugh that somehow seems to be sheltering grief and responsibility. Altogether different from Fridze's carefree grin.

Then last but not least, Gene. Handsome, tall, polished, slick, but somehow, behind the sophistication, a small boy is ever waiting to come to light. Blue eyes full of mystery and daring. But a shy something or other in his kiss, as if he is half afraid, half glad, half shy. All together, he gives the impression of a small boy that one would want to mother. Totally different from Micky's serious, masterful character.

They are all so different, and when I picture them in my mind, one by one, they seem to parade before me. I wonder which, say 10 years from now, will be the most successful businessman.

Sunday, September 27
Nothing happened. I kept thinking of a cute little boy today.

Monday, September 28
Micky was so indifferent. I don't understand it. I didn't see Gene today.

Tuesday, September 29
Oh, Micky was wonderful. He walked down the hall with me and was *so* nice. Oh, I like him so. I saw Gene today, and he said, "Hello, Doris." So cute. But he certainly don't look 17. As I said before, he reminds me of a little boy that I'd like to kiss. Not as a boy kisses a girl but as a mother kissing a child. He reminds me so much of a timid little baby. Not sissified at all. But oh, I can't explain it. He isn't the type I could ever fall madly in love with and get. It's something—oh, I don't know, I give up.

I wish Jack would call me up.

After I had written this, I went to bed and had just gotten in when Jack called. Isn't that funny? Just about the time I wish he would call, he nearly always does. I guess it's a case of "Two minds with but a single thought."[25] I like him awfully well. He's so clever and yet flattering in the things he says. Dad made me quit talking to him tonight, tho. Oh heck, such is life. I like three boys real well now. I wonder which will stand the longest. BAH. I'm a sentimental fool.

---

[25] Julius and Agnes Zancig were stage magicians and "mentalists" billed as "Two minds with but a single thought" from the 1880s to 1916.

Wednesday, September 30

Micky was awfully nice today. He acted so cute during English class. I think he really likes me. That isn't being conceited or anything, but oh, I don't know. Today when I came into class, I realized that I'd left my compact upstairs. I told the teacher I had left my English book in my locker, and she said I could get it if I would hurry. So I dashed out, grabbing my books from my desk as I went. I glanced back, and Micky was looking after me with a worried frown on his face. Of course I stayed away as long as possible, and when I came back, he looked so relieved. He said he was afraid my class had been changed. Oh boy, that shows that he *must* like me *just a little*.

Fanny, Gene, Joe, and I all rode up on the same [street]car today. When we got on top of the hill, Fanny and Gene came over. We danced and had a gay old time. When Joe took Fanny home, I asked Gene what he thought of her. He said that she was all right, but she wasn't his type. He said that if there was anything a boy hated, it was being so darn emotional like she was. He said, "Now Marjie is different. She's peppy without getting so silly." We talked in an impersonal way for a whole hour about different types of girls and et cetera.

He told me the kind he liked and didn't like. I know it sounds silly saying all this, but it's just to show what our friendship is going to be like. I'll bet within a month, he will be just like a brother. He wanted to know what I thought of the girl I saw him with today and seemed to really consider my opinion. Gosh, it's lucky I don't like him like I do Jack Freidel, or I would be in misery. He's raving about other girls. In our confident[ial] talk, he said that Fanny would probably object to a little kissing or *mugging*, as he called it. He said, "Now I don't mean that I want to mug all the time. But I like a girl that you can kiss once in a while without getting slapped or without her getting too hard."[26] My, it's nice to be able to talk to a boy that way. I'll bet we do get to be real good friends in time to come.

---

26 Gene means coarse or embittered.

Thursday, October 1

Micky was awfully nice today, but somehow I don't like him as well as I did. Gene, Joe, and I went to Fanny's this afternoon. They have a beautiful home. You know, I don't think I particularly like anybody now. I just woke up to the fact today. It's been an awful long time since my heart has gone bounding forward at a word or look from some boy. I wonder if I'm getting too old or what. I'd like to be in love again for a change. I think I would feel that way with Jack Freidel if I could only see him. Oh, I know I've been talking on the phone with him, but somehow that isn't just the same. And even then, I doubt if he could thrill me. There is just one boy that I *know* could.

I realized that the day I went to Grant, but didn't say anything about it because the girls would have laughed. I suppose it's silly. I've known him for two years, and yet when he passed me in the hall at Grant, I experienced that quick turning of my heart that is so wonderful. I must not have any pride at all, for even considering the silly way I once acted, and considering the way he acted that last night. If he would only make one little move or advance toward me, I would fly right to him. He passed by me that day without the least sign of recognition. I wonder if he felt like I did inside. Probably not.

Oh, I'd give the world right now if I could claim him as I once did. I've never admitted all this before. I've always acted like I didn't care, but I do. Oh, when I think of him, my heart aches so terribly. Oh [scribbled out]. (I'm not mentioning his name because I'm afraid someone sometime might read this. But oh, I love him so.)

Friday, October 2

I skipped school and went over to Grant today. In the hall I passed right by *him*. His shoulder brushed my arm, and he turned, said "Pardon me," and walked on as if he had never met me before. Oh, it nearly broke my heart. I wanted to sit right down and weep. But my spirits began to rise when I saw Jack Freidel. He's awfully cute and has the most tantalizing smile.

Gene and Fanny came over this afternoon. While they were here, Jack F. called up. I used to think I was wild about him, but since I've been thinking of *the* Him—oh, I love him so. When his shoulder touched mine, electric shocks went through my whole being, and my knees began to shake. And when he turned and looked me full in the eye without the least sign of recognition, it was awful. I thought I would die and had to walk right along with Marjie and keep a straight face. I don't dare tell the girls the way I feel about him for they would kid the life out of me. I suppose it *is* silly, but *then, oh!!!*

Saturday, October 3
Gene came over tonight. I don't like him, and yet I do, in a way. Fanny was over. He don't like her at all, I know, and he acted as if he liked me. But he's too childish to suit me. Too youngish, even though he is seventeen. He kisses *so* funny. So bashfully. I—oh, heck.

Sunday, October 4
~~I hate Gene. Yes, I do, too. He's so conceited and foolish. He acts like a little kid about 15. There isn't anything to him. He's so shallow and dry. Bah! I hate him, I do, I do, I do.~~

He isn't so bad. I was just prejudiced for a while, I guess. He told me I had pretty eyes.

Monday, October 5
Gene and Fanny were up this afternoon. Jack Freidel phoned, and Gene listened in. He's a darn fool, he is, by heck. Micky was awfully nice. I believe I like him, but after all, that is, of course, not counting The HIM.

Tuesday, October 6

Micky gets nicer every day. He does. The better I know him, the better I like him. There's so much to him. He thinks about something besides necking and mugging all the time.

Wednesday, October 7

I went to the foot ball game today. Lincoln won, 7–0. Micky's brother talked to me all during the game.

Thursday, October 8

My, of all that has happened today. First of all, Micky was wonderful. During lunch period he was sitting with the boys in the assembly. They pointed at me several times and seemed to be talking about me. Then one of the boys got up and started towards me. Micky pulled him back. Then the other boy held Micky while this one came up to me. He said, "Do you know a boy by the name of Micky Stevens?" Then he wanted to know what I thought about him and everything. Of course I wouldn't tell him, but it was interesting anyway. Tonight Gene came over, and Jack phoned up. Jack was nicer than he has ever been before. Oh, I love him so. He has such a nice manly voice and the brilliant laugh—oh —

Friday, October 9

Today, Micky said to me, "What did that milk-faced jelly fish say to you yesterday?" I told him, and he said, "Well, I just want you to know that he is[n't] any friend of *mine*. I don't associate with those kind of people." Oh boy.

Oh, say, the [cutest] boy moved across the street today. Gene promised to give Fanny and me [a knock down?] to him tomorrow.

Saturday, October 10

This is Saturday afternoon, but I haven't anything else to do, so I might as well write. You know, it's funny, but I keep thinking of Fridze. I don't know why. I was never particularly crazy about him. And yet, I keep thinking of his big eyes and ever-ready smile. I'd love to see him. I dreamed about him last night, and he's in my mind constantly. It's kind of uncanny. I have the funniest ache in my throat when I think of him. He's so sunny and boyish—oh, I ought to be thinking of Micky cause I like him best, but every time I try to picture Micky in my mind, Fridze crowds him out. I don't understand it at all.

**Doris's mother, in the backyard of the 1320
Alameda Avenue house, circa 1918.**

It's nearly 12 o'clock now (NIGHT), and my, of all I've been through. I guess I'll start at the beginning. Virginia Venerable invited all four of us kids to her party. Mother said that I *could not* go. Fannie's mother said that she *could not* go. But Joe and Gene could. Of course, that was tough, so we planned that Gene and Fanny were to come over that night (Mother and Dad were going to be out). Then the boys would take us to the party and get us home before Mother did. Fanny and me were real excited about it because it was a so-called "tough" party. Everything was going to work out fine, and then—the boys went back on us. They just wouldn't take us. They said that they didn't want to get back before twelve [midnight] and simply walked off and left us. Mad? Oh, I was so mad.

After we had fumed around for a while, we decided to go by ourselves. Even if it wasn't proper. We hunted all over town before we found the place (about 9 o'clock) and went in. Of course the boys were surprised, but we just snubbed them. And when they asked how we were going to get home, we told them that John Leon and another boy was going to meet us. The party began to get awfully tough, so we decided to leave. We told them that our "dates" were waiting just around the corner and were going to take us up to "Hill Villa."[27]

Both of them looked rather worried when we left, and believe me, they had cause for worry. We had just gotten down by the Central Library when we discovered that a couple of drunkards were following us. This didn't scare us much because they were so far behind. But in crossing a street, we had to stop to let a streetcar pass. They caught up and passed us. Just as they passed, Fanny said, "My, we aren't *very* stewed, are we?" I guess they thought we were trying to flirt because they turned, and it was then that we discovered only one was stewed. The other was holding the other up. They were about 22 years old and real good looking. The drunk one had his hat tipped way over on one side of his head. Well, anyway, when he turned and looked at us, he grinned the most terrible grin. Fanny and I turned heel and ran. The men followed us three whole blocks. Finally we lost them, but oh, it was awful. A regular nightmare. Gee, but we were scared.

---

27 Hill Villa was a Portland restaurant known for its fine cuisine. It is called The Chart House today.

Sunday, October 11

Gene came over today. Oh, I hate him so. He's positively awful. Conceited, ugh. Oh, I hate the very thought of him.

Monday, October 12

I love Micky. I know I do. He's so steadfast and sure. There isn't any danger of him getting uppish and awful. I HATE EUGENE.

Tuesday, October 13

Micky is so nice.

Wednesday, October 14

I just love Micky. No, I don't either, but I like him better than—*like*—and yet I don't guess I love him. Every time I see him, I have such a comfortable, happy feeling. We almost had a fight today, and when he saw that I was getting mad, he took some bold steps all right. I wasn't really mad, but I just wanted to see how he would act if I did get mad. Lloyd and Perry are coming up Saturday. Gee, it will be good to see them.

Thursday, October 15

Oh, I like Micky. Today I asked him how I could get to [the] Multnomah Club.[28] I was going to the foot ball game and he said, "I'll take you up there." Um. He did, too. He looked so cute, but the only thing wrong was that he had to smoke a cigarette. Oh, how I hate them. He looked awfully cute while smoking, but then that doesn't excuse him in the least. Oh, heck. Jack called me up tonight. He's cute as the dickens. I like him so.

---

28 An exclusive, private social and athletic club in Portland, founded in 1891.

Friday, October 16

Micky sat with me in Assembly. I'm progressing. Oh! What?

Saturday, October 17

Oh gosh! Perry and Lloyd came up tonight. It was good to see them all right. Gene came over, too. I tried to get Fanny to come over, but she couldn't—so I was left alone with the boy. Of course I had piles of fun. Three boys to flirt with. It was an opportunity I didn't miss. Gene and me acted awfully silly. We fought (not seriously), and he pulled my hair, then he would grab me in his arms and dance. He acted so silly that I decided I would, too.

He pretended like he was Rudolph Valentino and, oh, I don't know. He acted awfully funny. I can't get over it. First he would say, "You're no good." Then if I should dance with Lloyd, he'd yank me away. Anyway, he chased me out on the porch once, and we were scuffling around. I think he was trying to make me take back something I had said or something. I've forgotten. Anyway, we were scuffling on the terrace, and all of a sudden he seemed to get stronger. He pinned my arms to my side, and I looked up to see what it was all about.

His face was deathly white, and he grabbed me and pressed his lips to mine so tight and savagely, I was scared. I've never experienced that feeling before. His kisses have always been so timid and shy like a small boy. But the way he squeezed me and held me so tight, I couldn't breathe. And the kiss was *so* long. I had the funniest feeling in my spine. I was never so surprised in all my life because he had been acting so silly, and his kiss was so passionate and full of feeling. When he first grabbed me, I struggled to free myself, but it was useless.

Anyway, when he finally *did* release me, I was so stunned I just staggered back against the wall and stared at him. He looked at me a minute (his face was still white, and the muscles in it were tense). He said, "You little devil," and stalked into the house. I *can't* understand it.

43

Sunday, October 18
Nothing happened. Dull day.

Monday, October 19
Nothing happened. Dull day.

Tuesday, October 20
Today before school I was talking to Micky's chum, and he said that Micky was simply wild about me and terribly jealous. Every time that he would so much as mention me, Micky would get mad. Of course, that was good news to me, so I decided to make him real jealous. During English I just raved about Harold, and Micky (darling) took it all in. He got terribly mad, and when he walked down the hall with me, he didn't speak until we got to my room. Then he said, "I'll have to look Harold up," and beat it.

Of course, I dashed into the room and told Harold all about it, and he thought it was a huge joke and agreed to carry it through. He said that he "would rave about me and we'd have some sport with him."

I didn't see either of them until lunch period in the Assembly. Micky sat across the aisle with another boy, and Harold came in. Harold saw me and Micky—winked and came and sat with me. He leaned over and made believe he was simply wild about me. Out of the corner of my eye I could see Micky. Oh, but he looked mad. Well—all went well, and I went to the game after school. Micky was sitting close to Gene. I was sitting with Marjie. When the game was over, Micky and Gene came over and walked out with us. Micky was kind of sullen (it made him look so cute), and when I mentioned Harold, his eyes just flamed. He glared at me and changed the subject. He walked to the car line with me. Oh, I can't wait til tomorrow. I wrote a poem about Harold, and I don't know whether to show it to Micky or not. I don't want to go too far.

Wednesday, October 21

I showed Micky the poem, and boy, but he was mad. Harold sat with me again in assembly, and Micky just glared. Jack called up tonight.

Monday, October 26

It's been a long time since I've written. Nothing much has happened except I don't think I like Micky anymore.

Tuesday, October 27

Gee, enough has happened today. While I was down in the gym, I ran into an iron bar. It hit my nose, threw me back on my head, and knocked me unconscious. They carried me up to the Dean's office, and my, but I got a lot of attention. At lunch period, all the girls flocked in and everything. Finally, I was taken home, and the doctor came tonight. He thinks my nose is broken but can't tell until tomorrow because it is so swollen. And I am a sight. My nose is spread all over my face, and my head is aching so. I don't think that I've ever suffered such pain before. It's terrible.

Wednesday, October 28

The inside of my nose is bent all out of shape, and maybe I'll be operated on tomorrow. Alas, who knows. I got a whole bunch of letters today from the kids. It seems that the whole school knows about my accident. Margret said that she told Micky and that he was terribly worried. He might write me tomorrow, but I doubt it. Oh, wouldn't it be simply sublime if he did? I would be in the seventh heaven of joy. My, but I'm silly to even think of such a thing, but I just can't help hoping.

Saturday, November 21

Well! Here it is November, and I haven't written in nearly a month! I went to a Hill Military[29] party tonight, and oh, but I had fun. I'll start at the beginning. First, we all congregated in the dressing room. The girls, I mean. Then we went down single file through a long lot of dark hallways. Finally we came out upon a porch, and from there we went into the Armory. It was so funny. At the back they had three pinto horses, two sheep, a bunch of chickens, and two calves fenced off.

It was all so exciting, and then we got our partners for the grand march. Mine looked exactly like Jack Pillar, and every time I looked at him, my knees nearly refused to hold me. We marched to one side of the room, and the flag came in. The boys all stood at salute, and I glanced right-ways at my partner. Oh, I got a thrill. His eyes were straight ahead, and he looked so serious. Then we danced, and danced, and danced. Then the second dance began, and I danced with the adorablest [*sic*] little big blond. He was easy to talk to, and we got along fine. I was describing a boy, and I said, "Not bad looking." "I'll say you're not," he said. Of course, that made me feel great.

I asked him to introduce me to some of the boys, which he did. By heck, they were all blonds. "Good Lord," I thought. "Doesn't this school believe in brunettes?" Then we bumped into a couple—"Excuse us, Thacker," said my partner. I turned around, and it was a brunette. "Oh, Don," I said. "Introduce me to that boy, won't you?" "Sure," he said.

At the end of the first half, Don took me over to him and introduced me. "I'll trade you dances, Don," Thacker said, and they did. I was in the seventh heaven of joy, and then the whistle blew for us to clear the floor. Mad! Oh, I was mad. Anyway, we went over and sat on the fence. He was easy to talk to, tho, and cute as heck, so my spirits began to rise. Four boys

---

29 Hill Military Academy, opened in 1901, was a private, college-preparatory military academy in Portland. It closed in 1959.

came forward and received some badges. Then a flash light picture[30] was taken, and we were ready to dance.

The other boys hadn't been very good dancers, and I was hoping with all my heart that this one would be good. He took me in his arms, and I held my breath. I did so want him to be a good dancer. Then we started. I needn't have had any fears. He started out like a professional—and pep! Say, he was brimming over with it. He was wonderful, divine, marvelous, exquisite, and I fitted in his arms like a glove. We fairly raced across the floor, and he was so *easy* to follow. I was so excited, I gave a squeal of delight. He looked down at me (I forgot to say he's real tall), he looked down at me and laughed. "Like it?" he asked. "Do I!" I said, and then I raved. I've never danced with anyone that was so heavenly and told him so like a little fool. He only laughed, tho, and we danced some more.

Young friends of the Bailey family take a few dance steps in front of the house, circa 1920.

---

30 Flash photo.

He told me how wonderfully I followed and everything, but of course he did that just to be polite. But oh, he danced marvelously fast, slow, hop, step, side. I have often wondered about how some girls could rave about the way boys danced. They always seemed the same to me. I see my mistake now. Then we ate refreshments. We had to go to the porch to get to the kitchen, and when we went across, I shivered. "Cold?" he asked, and put his arm around me. That was the only thing he did all evening like that. I guess that's why I liked him so well. And even then, he wasn't in the least bit suggestive or anything. Only kind of protective. Then we all sat on tables and ate our ice cream. After that we all gathered around the piano and sang. Gee, it was nice. Then we went back to dance.

I had forgotten how divinely he danced, and when he took me in his arms, I was positively giddy. I know I danced better then than I ever had in my life because I was so marvelously happy. Then something happened. Nearly everyone cleared away to the sides except a few, and we were left alone in the middle. When we finished, everyone clapped. Um!!! Finally, it was time to go home, and oh, how I hated to leave.

Monday, November 30
I showed Micky a poem today about love. The last lines were these: "Yet the light of a whole life dies when love is done."[31] He was wonderful, said he agreed with it and everything. Then I began to rave about Harold, and he got kind of mad. Third period I saw him walking down the hall with Bernice Hamilton. I was so mad I felt like I could chew nails. He was gazing down into her beautiful blue eyes, and he didn't even *see* me. Damn Bernice. She's just a heartless little flirt. Micky means nothing to her while he is my life, my soul. The means of my very existence. Life holds nothing for me now. I shall have to close the doors of my heart, bury my love in a remote corner, and forget him. Oh, how can I?

---

31 From the poem, "The Night Has a Thousand Eyes," by Francis William Bourdillon, 1878.

It seems impossible, but I will, I will, I WILL. If he likes her, I'm just out of luck.

Tuesday, December 1

Well, things have gone from bad to worse. Micky just glared at me during English. I smiled at him, and he sat there without changing his expression in the least. It disturbed me, so I turned my attention to Steven, who sits across the aisle. Finally, Mrs. Haskins [Hankins?] said, "Steven, you must pay attention to the lesson and not quite so much to Doris."

When the period was over, Steven walked out with me. Later I saw Micky talking to Bernice. Damn, damn, double damn. I wish I were dead.

Friday, December 4

I don't know what to make of life. Everything is full of hope. One minute Micky is nice, and then he'll suddenly shut up. I can't understand it.

Monday, December 14

I haven't written for a week because matters haven't made any progress. I'm just where I was two weeks ago except perhaps that I like Micky about five times as much as is good for me. I can't understand his attitude. He is so over-polite and seems so far away from me. I have a feeling that I have lost him forever.

Tuesday, December 15

Micky was so aloof today. I feel my heart getting heavier and heavier within me.

Wednesday, December 16

When Micky looks at me, I feel as if he were trampling my very soul beneath his feet. I can't understand it.

Thursday, December 17

I had lots of fun today. Paul Kenny was especially nice. But I want Micky.

Friday, December 18

Gosh, of all that has happened.

Margret, Lloyd, Gene, and Joe and me had a kind of party tonight. In fact, it was a regular necking party, and I feel terribly ashamed of myself for how we all acted. Anyway, that is neither here nor there. A great mystery has been cleared up this evening, and yet I'm not so sure whether it *has* been cleared up. Yes, I think it really complicates matters. Anyway, it is this.

Gene said tonight, "Say, Doris, I had some fun with your beloved Micky last week. You know what I did?"

Of course, at the first mention of Micky, I was all attention. "Tell me," I said.

"Well, I told him you went into Multnomah Club on the last half of girls' day and that you looked in the tank and saw him swimming." (The boys are nude when they swim.[32]) "You told me all about it.

"'Honest, did she?' Micky gasped.

---

[32] Boys commonly swam in the nude in clubs such as the YMCA and Multnomah, as well as in lakes and rivers. But they wore suits if girls were present, as at The Oaks.

"'Yes, and she told us kids all about it.' (Gosh, you should have seen his face!)

"'Well, that settles her for me. Here I was falling madly in love with her, and now I'll have to quit. Oh, of course I'll be a gentleman and all that, but I'll steel myself against her.'"

While Gene was narrating all this to me, I felt an icy hand clutch my heart. Why, no wonder he acted so queerly. Any boy would. Oh, what shall I do? I can't go tell him because he'd hate me more for bringing up the subject, and I can't talk to him about a thing like that. Oh.

Bathing beauties show off their bathing suits poolside at The Oaks, June 1918.

1926

[no date]

I haven't written for ages and ages. I'm going to forget everything that went on in the previous pages.

I might add that I have made up with Micky, and all is as [it] should be.

Tuesday, January 26

Life worries me. And so does love. I've just been talking to Alyce, and we've had our annual squabble about Marjie. I like Marjie, always have and always will. I like Alyce, always have and always will. And it's so strange that these two girls who I am so fond of dislike each other so intensely. Alyce says that Marjie's reputation at Grant is poor. In fact, it is nothing, and she (Alyce) will not be seen with Marjie else her reputation will go kerflunk. What can I do about it?

Alyce says that last summer when everyone dropped Marjie, I allowed her to tag along with me. I've made such a fool of myself, I suppose. And yet, I don't know. I myself can't see anything wrong with her. She's always been a good sport and has never done anything *really* wrong. *Oh hell*. I don't know what to do. Life is a problem.

I wish I could go away. Far, far away into the wilderness, where one would not always have to be worrying about one's reputation. I'm sick and tired of the whole DAMN business. I wish I could be just like everyone wants me to be. You can't, it seems, please everybody.

But Hell's bells, what can I do? I've planned a hike for next Thursday. I want Micky, Joe, Gene and Jack Pillar, me, Gladys, Marjie, and Alyce. But Alyce won't go if Marjie goes, and Marjie won't go if Alyce goes. They are both such good sports and so much fun that I want both. Even if I did leave one out, the other would be terribly offended.

Life is a farce. I think I'll run away from it all. DAMN IT.

Thursday, January 28

I'm thoroughly disgusted with boys. This is what happened. Marjie, Alyce, me, Joe, Gene, and Micky all went on a hike today. Everything started peachy. Micky walked with me, and we went way up in the woods for about a mile. Then Gene dared me to climb over an embankment that would cut off [half a] mile. Of course I accepted, and we went stumbling down. We walked about a mile before we came upon Micky, and then of course I was anxious to see who he was walking with. I wanted it to be Marjie because I trusted her. Alas, it was Alyce. She was flirting with him for dear life. I ignored them and kept walking with Gene. We walked miles and miles and miles and miles.

Finally we came upon the most adorable little log cabin, furnished and everything. The boys crawled in through the cooler and opened the door for us. I've never seen such a cute house. There were furs and stuff on the wall. All kinds of rustic furniture and an adorable chaise lounge. There was a kitchen with stove, cupboards, dishes, et cetera. Even a pantry with canned meat and fruit. It was like a fairy tale. Micky built a fire in the fireplace, pulled the chaise lounge up in front of the fire, and sat down. Immediately Alyce plopped down beside him and put her head on his shoulder.

Quick as a flash, his arm went around her, and she snuggled up against him. I could just stand there and stare. A terrible horror was creeping up into my heart. I was astounded that she, whom I consider a friend, would deliberately do that to him, who she knew was mine. I went into the kitchen and fumbled with the utensils. I felt as one in a dream. I was seriously considering going to them and forcing them apart. Then Gene saved my life. He came in the kitchen and flirted with me. Dear old Gene. I awoke myself and realized that I must carry on the bluff. So I flirted with him. Dinner passed, and the day wore on. Still Alyce sat on his lap. They sat in the corner and cooed like two love birds.

Slowly my anger gave way to disgust. My dreams began to fall. Here was this boy, whom I had idealized as a man of the west. A boy who symbolized all which was clean and noble. He, of all people, was stooping to the common, cheap vulgar means of kissing. PETTING. Oh, I was so disappointed that he had not turned out to be as I had idealized him that I went upstairs to powder my nose.

~~I had just shut the bedroom door when he came in. He stalked over to me and tried to kiss me. Finally he did. Instead of the thrill I expected to receive, a [sickening nearly?] came over me. I felt stifled and I wanted to slap him. I was so thoroughly, utterly disgusted that instead of flying into a rage, I gave him one look and stamped out of the room, and slammed the door. To think that he would sit all day on a chair and pet one girl, then to turn to me and kiss me. It was so vile. So vulgar.~~

Now the day has ended, and I'm disappointed in all mankind. I don't think that there is a nice, clean boy living.

Friday, January 29
At school today I was talking to Tilly and Joe. A voice came up from behind me and said, "Hello, Doris," right in my ear. At the sound of that voice, all happiness fled. Memory of yesterday swept over me. I knew without turning who it was, so I didn't turn, just went right on talking to Tilly. Finally I turned to go.

Fred Yarnell came up the steps two at a time. His eyes were dancing, and his face looked so clean and boyish, so unstained with cheap superfluous kisses. The contrast was so striking. I can't see how I ever liked that fool.

By the way, I flunked four subjects, so Mother is going to send me to S.H.H.[33] Can you beat it?

---

[33] St. Helen's Hall. In 1869, the Oregon Episcopal School (OES) was founded in downtown Portland, with the women-only St. Helen's Hall. OES is still extant.

**Mystery man: This photo was found secreted behind another photo
and has not been identified. Could this be Micky? Or Jack?**

Sunday, February 14

Oh, I'm happy, happy. Dear diary, how, oh how can I explain it? I don't
know how to say it. I don't even know what it is. What I mean is that I'm
in love. In love as I've never been before. I can see or think of nothing but
Jack. Yes, his name is Jack. It's getting to be a family tradition. Every boy
I've ever been awfully in love with has been a Jack.[34] This makes the sixth,
but oh! I'll start at the beginning.

I went to a Junior Prom with Johnny last night. We called in his car for
Evaline and Frenchy. Had a pretty good time, and Evaline came home with
me. Today a bunch of "Hill" boys that she knew phoned and wanted to

---

34 Her youngest brother was also nicknamed Jack.

come up. They came, six of them, and one's name was Jack Hibbard. You know the rest—one look at him and I knew I was a goner.

Not that he is so terribly good looking; still, he doesn't hurt your eyes in the least. He has straight black hair, blue eyes, a Greek nose, and a firm mouth. The only really good-looking part of him is his teeth. White and even. Gee, I like him. He was awfully easy to talk to, and everything was spiffy. Of course, the others were all good looking, but he was the only one I could see. When I danced with him, a funny little thrill would go up and down me. I liked him oh so well. And I think that he liked me.

He was so flatteringly attentive, too. Everything that I'd say, he would listen so closely to. Then I was trying to make him dance with one of the unpopular girls. "No," he said. "I'd much rather dance with you." But I refused to dance with him and held my hands tight at my sides. He forced my hands away and took me by main force and danced with me.

It's so funny, but I've never been thrilled before by a boy's dancing with me, but the pressure of his arm around my waist and the thought that he was so close to me just sent little thrills up and down my spine. Then I went in to make some candy. He followed me in and put a dish towel around his waist for an apron. He looked so adorably sweet that I wanted to kiss him. Just too cute for words. He beat the eggs and fussed around the kitchen. I told him to get the butter from the ice box, and he said, "All right, Darling." I was *so* excited.

We have a new record which is called "I've Got Some Lovin' to Do."[35] It's awfully cute, and I was singing it to myself.

"I have, too," he said. "We'll have to get together on that." Then he stared straight into my eyes without the ghost of a smile.

---

[35] "I've Got Some Lovin' to Do," Fred Waring and the Pennsylvanians, 1926.

My heart began to pound, and just then the door opened, and Gene came in. "Here, here, what's going on in here?" he said. Oh, I was so mad. He stayed for ages and then finally went out.

"As I was saying—" Jack began, and then [Doris's brother] Joe walked in.

"Pardon, pardon for intruding," he said, and walked out.

Jack smiled and came over to me, laid his hand on mine, and Rae and Mother came in. I was so disgusted. They stayed and stayed, and he never did get to finish what he started. Damn it all, anyway. Finally the candy was finished, and finally it was time for him to go.

"I'll phone sometime next week," he whispered in my ear as he went out. Oh, I love him so.

Monday, February 15
Today was uneventful. I couldn't get my mind off Jack.

Tuesday, February 16
Today I was in combing my hair, and I mentioned Jack's name to Evaline. One of the girls overheard me and said, "Oh, do you mean Jack Hibbard?" I nodded, and she said, "For goodness sakes, don't get too thick with him if you want to save your self respect."

"Oh, he's perfectly gentlemanly to me," I said. "He hasn't done anything to reprove, that I know of."

"That's all right. I'm just warning you to watch your step. I've had experience with him, and I know. He isn't all that he pretends to be."

That was all, but it has worried me all day. I don't know why. Heck, I hope he *is* all right.

I saw Micky down town today. He stopped and talked, but oh, how I hate him. He was so dissipated looking. And no character whatsoever in his face. How I ever liked him is a miracle to me.

Wednesday, February 17
Nothing happened. Uneventful day.

Thursday, February 18
Oh, boy. I can't wait until tomorrow. I'm going over to Evaline's, and *Jack* is going to be there.

This is the diary of
Doris Bailey. Age
sixteen years.
Beginning March 14. 1926

Thursday, March 11

I decided to change books because the other one was so terribly full. I am 16 years old today and thought my birthday was as good a time as any to change. I've left out about a month, and lots has happened during that time. I want to forget most of it, so I'm going to pretend that it just didn't happen. Now that everything has been explained, I can begin. Ahem!!

I don't feel any older than I did yesterday. But I am. I'm 16. Gee, but that seems funny.

Friday, March 12

Jack came up tonight. He looked perfectly adorable and was so flattering. Everything was going fine. We took the Ford out and dragged Alyce and Gene along. We went for a long drive and finally parked in a lonesome, out of the way place. Then he kissed me. And *oh*, how wonderfully he kisses. I was happy, oh so happy. Then we came back. We danced a while, and then I noticed to my horror that Alyce was flirting with him. He pulled her down on his lap and grinned at her. I felt myself get hot and cold. Oh, she couldn't, she wouldn't do a thing like that. She had done it with Micky, but I thought she had learned her lesson after that.

Nevertheless, she hadn't, and I was just sick. You know the rest. It turned out just like that damned hike. I'm so heartsick. I can hardly live. I don't see how she could do a thing like that. And yet she has the nerve to call herself my friend. Oh!!

Saturday, March 13

I went to the Hill [Military Academy] dance tonight, and Fun? Say, I've never had so much fun in *all my life*. The boys were so nice, and if I do say it myself, I think I was popular. I danced every dance and had to refuse pecks of them. I snubbed Jack good until the last dance, and then coldly consented to dance with him. I ate with Bob Stryker and had a *wonderful* time. "Frenchy" begged for me to let him come up, and George Hanson asked for a date. One boy came up to me and said, "Aren't you Doris Bailey?"

"Yes," I said. "How'd you guess it?"

"Oh. When you were eating with Bob, some of the boys told me who you were. They talked about you all the time you were eating."

Of course I wanted to know what they said, but I couldn't appear too interested, so I didn't ask him. He must have read my thoughts, tho, because he said, "Don't worry. It was all complimentary." Umm, that means that they are taking an interest.

One boy said that he had seen me lots of times before but hadn't had the nerve to ask me to dance. Still another said that I was the only girl he'd danced with that could *dance*. Ahem!

Young people in a boat on the Willamette River.

Sunday, March 14

Oh la la. Talk about fun. Say, today sure took the cake. I went out to Marjie's, and we went for a sailboat ride. It's an experience that I would never miss for anything. The swirling, dimpling Willamette[36]—oh! To glide serenely over the sunlit waters with nary a care in the world. Then to have the wind suddenly change and the sails flap and blow like big white birds. The moment of suspense when the boat wavers on the edge of destruction, and then peace once more. There is a something that gets into your spirit. A wild, untamable something when you feel that you are trusting your life to a piece of canvas and a raft. But I haven't reached the climax yet. When we came in sight of the raft, who should I see but *Fridzi*. My heart bounded ahead, and I just stared. *Fridzi*, of all people. I hadn't seen him for nearly a year and was oh so happy. He waved to me, and then we came to shore.

His eyes were just as pretty and his lashes prettier. He was so nice, and we decided to take a canoe ride. We went way down by the bridge and talked and talked and talked. He was so cute and finally came and sat down with me in the middle. I recited poetry to him, and then he kissed me. He had improved immensely since last summer, and I was actually THRILLED. He is so cute. Oh, oh, oh. Of course I know that he doesn't have a very good reputation, but it was exciting just the same. Alyce needn't think she is so damn smart about taking Micky and Jack. I can get them also. And Fridzi is 19 years old and not the least bit juvenile. I like him. I don't care, I do.

Wednesday, March 17

Oh, I'm so mad, mad, mad, mad to think that I am treated this way. Oh, just imagine this. I went out three nights last week, and there was nothing wrong with that. Last night I went down to the store to buy a high school [note]pad. I didn't tell Mother because she would have said it wasn't proper.

---

36 The Willamette River is a tributary of the Columbia River; both rivers flow through Portland: the Willamette through downtown, the Columbia to the north.

But I had to get it so I could get a theme [essay] in. If it wasn't in, I would have been in the deficiency list, and I hated to disappoint Mother again, so I went without asking. Of course, they were simply furious. When I got back, they wouldn't believe me when I told them that it was absolutely necessary. They nearly had a fit because I tried to please them. Of course, that was bad enough, but just now Alyce phoned and wanted me to come up for the weekend. I asked Mother, and she said NO, absolutely I could not go outside of the house this weekend. Furthermore, I could not have a new suit and blah! blah! blah!

After I work all week long trying to make good grades, and then they act that way. I think I need a little recreation after slaving all week, and you'd think they would be willing to give it to me but no. For all they care, I could work 8 hours a day, and they wonder why it wasn't 10. Damn it!! If they think keeping me in is going to make me any sweeter, they have another "think" coming. It's the injustice of it that hurts. You'd think I was a step child. Damn, damn, damn. Oh! I'm so mad. I'm through!! I'm going to skip out. They are crushing the youth out of me. I'm only 16 and they want me to act 100. Can't go out ever! If I even smile, or look happy, they bawl me out. My mind isn't even my own.

Mother manages all my affairs, and I'm just a mere piece of machinery. You'd think that they would be satisfied putting me in a girls' school, shutting away from me all that I love, but they aren't. It's just one damn fight after another. I hate it all, and I'm going to run away.

Thursday, March 18
Dull day. Nothing happened.

Friday, March 19
Frank Seans[?] phoned and wanted me to go out with him tomorrow night. Of course, Mother wouldn't let me. Damn it all anyway.

Saturday, March 20

Played tennis with Fanny today. We walked below the hill to get a Sundae and saw Jack Hibbard. He's cute as hell but—oh, so fickle. Marjie came in for the weekend. Gene came over this evening and we discussed *Sicology*[37] (how do you spell it?). He has more horse-sense [common sense] than I first thought he had. Hmm!!

Sunday, March 21

Bob Stryker phoned and wanted to come up this evening. I had to study, tho—damn it. Just the same, I was terribly flattered. Not that I like him very well, but he's popular, and it's kind of nice to feel that he is getting interested. It means improvement, and *that's* something. I wish it had been Jack, tho. It always is that way. The ones I like don't pay me *any* attention, and those I'm not wild about do. Darn it!!

Monday, March 22

Stayed home from school today with a sore throat. Gee, but I wish something *real* exciting would happen.

---

37 Psychology.

Doris attended St. Helen's Hall, an Episcopal school for girls, as a day student.

Tuesday, March 23

Oh, but I hate school!! I stayed out just *one* day, and now I have so much to make up. Damn it. If I *only* had some decent clothes to wear, all would be well. I had to stay in tonight. When I did come, the conductor said that a bunch of Hill boys came up, but I wasn't home. Isn't that just *my* luck. As I said before, damn it!!

Wednesday, March 24

Well!! Jack Hibbard just phoned me up. He wanted to know why I was mad at him. He said that I dashed out of the dance Saturday night without even saying "goodby." I convinced him that I wasn't mad, and he said, "Well, then, can I come up Friday night?" I had intended [on] going to Alyce's, but of course I changed my mind in a second.

He said, "I'm going to bring Bob Stryker, so get another girl."

"How about Alyce?" I said.

"Who's that?"

"Oh, you know. The girl you enjoyed so much last Friday."

"Oh," he said. "She's all right. Bring her along."

We talked a while longer and then said goodby. In about half an hour Alyce phoned me and said that Jack phoned her and—well—made love to her[38] over the phone. He told her to be sure and be at my house Friday night.

Now what!!! can I make of that? He is so fickle and two-faced. I hate him!! Oh, I do, I do, and yet I love him!! What shall I do? I ought to call it off because he's coming for her, but oh, I want to see him so badly. Damn it!!

Thursday, March 25
Dull day—

Friday, March 26
Oh, gee. Everything was planned for Jack to come. Alyce and Bob were coming, too. I got to thinking [about] what Jack said about Alyce and got mad. I resolved not to see him ever again, so I went over to Alyce's for dinner. My conscience began to hurt me about 7 o'clock because it *was* kind of mean to run off and leave him like that. So I phoned HMA [Hill Military Academy] and told him that I was up at Alyce's. He was terribly mad, because he said he wanted to see me. He sounded so genuinely hurt that I forgave him and told him to come up to Alyce's. He said, "All right. Be up in about an hour." We hung around until 9:30. Then Hal and Walt came by and wanted us to go over to the church with them. We thought they weren't coming, so we went. We got home about 11:30 and found that the boys had come about 10:00. Damn!! Now I'll bet he *is* mad at me. Run away from him twice? *Damn!!* I'll bet he never speaks to me again as long as he lives.

---

38 She means he was romantic, not sexual. See glossary.

Saturday, March 27

Jack phoned and wants to come up tomorrow. Oh la la! He wasn't at all mad, either. I went to a party with John Painton tonight. Had a marvelous time, and I met the *cutest* boy. He looked just like Fritzi. There was another one there that looked like Ned. He was awfully nice to me. Still another said I had the "swellest" hair he'd ever seen, and another said I danced divinely. Bob Dick danced with me three times. All things considered, I had a marvelous time, as I said before.

Sunday, March 28

Oh, hell, hell, damnation. *Son of a seacook. I hate Jack.* He came up this afternoon. *So did Alyce.* He brought Tom Kennedy, too. Everything started out fine, and Jack was so nice. Then damn fool Alyce started her flirting. About 4 o'clock Bob Hibbard, Ross [Mindoll?], [and] John Dykme[?] came up. We made candy and fiddled around. I tried to be gay, but I didn't succeed. My heart was so heavy. I wanted to scream out in agony, and I had to smile quietly. Damn, damn, damn! I'm mad.

Then when he started to go, he patted my cheek, and I wanted to kiss and kick him. I hate him, yet I love him. DAMN Alyce anyway. She is determined to ruin my happiness. Oh, well. I've lost him for good now. That's evident. Not that I ever had him, but I was on the path. *DAMN.*

Bob was awfully nice, tho. He is so mannerly. So much of a gentleman. I like him. He put his arm around me once, and I was so thrilled. He's awfully good looking and has the beautifullest [*sic*] eyes I've ever seen. So deep and unfatholmess[39] [*sic*] and mysterious. They hide so many emotions. I'll bet he'll amount to something when *he* grows up.

---

[39] Fathomless.

Monday, March 29

I kept thinking of Micky today. His blue eyes and black hair. He is so much nicer than these superfluous sheiks. There is something *to* him. He has character and good sense. I love him. I know I do. He is always so serious and nice. So steadfast and sure. Like the rock of Gibraltar. He is *oh* so ideal. I'm getting sick of these other boys. There's nothing to them. Absolutely nothing there, slick black hair and cheap mugging. Ugh!! But, Micky, *oh* he's so clean, so afire with the joy of living. He never indulges in petting parties or drinking. Gee, but I like him.

Tuesday, March 30

We just had a choice family row. Mother found out that the boys acted wild and got into Daddy's gin, so they've been giving me hell. Joe, like the ~~damn~~ darn[40] fool he is, tried to say he had nothing to do with it, when in truth it was he that came up the stairs to get it. You would think that he had absolutely no honor at all. The ~~damn~~ darn fool.

Now I can't go to any more HMA dances. I can't go out with any Hill boys, and I can't have them up here. ~~Damn~~ Darn!! I can't even answer the phone and talk to them. Isn't that just plain Hell? Damn it all anyway. I'm mad!! Just when I was getting in good with them.

Wednesday, March 31

Dull day.

Thursday, April 1

Today was April Fool's Day. Awfully uneventful and dry. No school tomorrow.

---

[40] Doris apparently had misgivings about swearing in her diary; she edited and cleaned up several pages of swearing.

List of — well — ahem!!!!!!!
What would you call them?
Infatuations?

Blue eyes 7 — Lloyd — Washington
(how could I?)
grey eyes 4 — Perry — Blah!!! Booth — Grant — Secret sorrow
blue eyes 1 — Bruce Cambell — Milwaukee — Ben Crosby Grant
brown eyes 3 — Martin Allen — Grant High 3 — Cloton Caldwell (Grant)
Blue eyes 6 — Hal Paddock — Benson Alt — Leanord Blakly (Benson)
Blue eyes 3 — Malkom Mitchell ("Mickey") — Grant High 4 — Cecil — O.A.C. cute — !
Wonderful Eyes
Brown eyes — Jack Pillar — Grant High 5 — Jack ~~Frickel~~ Grant (few too short!)
Brown eyes 2 — Bob Ziegler — California High 6
grey eyes 8 — " Christians — Washington H 9 — Tonny Wenerosky
Grey eyes 9 — John Acton — Grant High — Fred Yarnell
brown eyes 1 — Jack Waldron — Lincoln High — Johny Goss
blue eyes 12 — Col Beaulander — Milwaukee H 14
marvelous eyes
grey eyes 10 — Freolrich (Friedji) (Benson) (awfully cute)
blue eyes 14 — (which) Jack Friedel — Grant — (the real one at last)
grey eye — 15 — Micky (oh so wonderful) Lincoln
blue eyes 16 — Gene Rosman (Banks) (adorable)
Well Military accademy — Loren (Shorty) (reeving dancer)
17 — Jack Ablard — I love him

Friday, April 2

Went to buy a suit with Alyce today. I bought it but don't think I like it. Will probably take it back. I'm getting lonesome for the Hill boys.

Saturday, April 3

Came out to Marjie Dana's today. Gee! But I love her.

Sunday, April 4

Went canoeing today with Marjie. While we were in the river, Bruce came up in his canoe. Then Kenny and Bob Richardson came up in the sailboat. They wanted us to get in with them, so we made Bruce take our canoe back and climbed into the sailboat. Had pecks of fun. Saw some boys in swimming with nothing on, but pretended not to because we were with Kenny and Bob. Marjie and me were struck with the giggles, tho, and it was terrible. Finally, the boys saw what we were laughing at and blushed profusely.

The funny part of it was that the naked boys weren't the least bit embarrassed. They just turned their backs on us and laughed. The situation was becoming unbearable until a gust of wind arose and blew us away.

Rae's friends getting dressed after a swim at the railroad bridge and swimming hole, Miami River, Tillamook County.

Monday, April 5

Didn't go to school today because I had a sore throat. I was down below the Hill about 3 o'clock, and the HMA boys were out drilling [marching]. As I passed, a bunch of them saluted. So cute. It made me so homesick for them. I wish I didn't have to cut them.

Tuesday, April 6

School is becoming terribly dry.

Wednesday, April 7

I hate school!!!

Thursday, April 8

Stayed home today and played tennis with Fanny.

Friday, April 9

No more school until a week from Monday. Hip hip horray [*sic*]! Spring vacation. I met Marjie down town, and she came home with me. Gene came over and made love to her. Gee, but he sure is bit hard.[41]

Saturday, April 10

Went swimming at the Nat[42] this afternoon. Keen sport. Came home with Marjie.

Sunday, April 11

Today Marjie and myself went up to Oregon City to rent some horses. They charged 50 cents an hour, and we both had a dollar apiece. That made only two hours, and we wanted to go for three. The stable boy was about 18 years old and a typical country hick, so we flirted another hour out of him. I had a wild horse and wild as the devil. We went out towards Canby[43] and rode and rode. I made Belle jump a creek, and once while we were racing, the stirrup broke. Another time I wanted him to walk, but he was too wild, and when I pulled him in, he reared up on his hind legs, and I slid off his back. It was fun, tho. When we went back, the stable boy said I was the best rider he'd ever seen. Umm.

Monday, April 12

Went to Milwaukee High School with Marjie today. Saw Fridzi. I don't like him anymore, tho. He's too shiekish looking and wears his hair too long. He was awfully nice to me, but—oh hell heck, he isn't refined enough to suit me. Too boisterous and all that sort of bunk. Even tho he is 19.

---

41 Bitten, meaning Gene has fallen for Marjie.
42 The Natatorium, a swimming pool.
43 South of Portland.

Tuesday, April 13
Went to Grant today. Had pecks of fun. I saw Jack Freidel, and he barely spoke to me. ~~Damn~~ Darn him. Oh well. I don't care. The other boys were real nice to me. I came home with Alyce. After dinner we were sitting on her front porch and trying to think of a plot for her story.

Two boys came up. One was Gordon Perry, and Alyce introduced the other as "Volmar Van Horn." Isn't that a peach of a name? Anyway, I saw in a minute that Alyce was wild about Volmar. I had been waiting for the chance to get even with her about Jack, and I realized that this was my opportunity, so I grabbed it. I flirted like hell with him, and it worked. Then I seated myself on a step below him and began reciting poetry. He fell like a ton of lead.

He began by telling me that I had wicked eyes and ended by asking for my phone number. After they had left, Alyce solemnly promised to leave my boy-friends alone ever afterwards if I wouldn't be home when he phoned. Poor kid. I gave her an awful scare, but she deserved it. I don't like Volmar and don't see how she could, but I'm glad she did. Now I'm safe with Jack.

Wednesday, April 14
I played tennis with Ruth and Maxine today. Just as I got to 23rd Street when I was coming home, a car full of HMA boys drove up and asked to take me up the hill. I went with them, and it was lots of fun. When they drove up with me, Mother stuck her head out of the window and looked so mad that they gave one glance and backed out like lightning, instead of coming in like they were going to. ~~Damn~~ Darn it all anyway. Something always happens to spoil my happiness.

I half-hoped that Volmar would phone tonight, but it's nine now, so I guess he doesn't intend to. I got a darling new suit the other day. A silk pleated blouse to go with it and everything.

Thursday, April 15

I went to Lincoln today and saw Fred Yarnell. Gee, he's cute as hell and then some.

Friday, April 16

Oh, I'm *so* mad. This evening about 9 o'clock, Dale, Marjie, and a boy I'd never met came over. He was awfully cute and mannerly. The folks were gone, but Joe[44] and Gene were here. We played the Victrola and danced. Then went in to make some candy. While we were in there, Gene and Joe took the crank to the Victrola. We went in to play it while the candy was cooking and found it gone. Then Joe took the candy off the stove. Also, they hid the cake. I was never so *mortified* in all my life. They acted like 12-year-old boys. Of course there was nothing left for us to do but sit on the couch and talk.

Then Joe and Gene began to cut-up. Everything that we would say, Gene would make some sarcastic comment. Oh, how I hate him. Dick said, "Do they always act that way?" I know that he must have thought they were half-wits or something. And it was so embarrassing to have my guest treated in that manner. Finally we could stand it no longer, so we went for a walk. It was rainy and disagreeable, tho, so we soon had to come back. They left around 11:30, and I know they must have been thoroughly disgusted. I'll never be able to face those boys again. Oh damnation son of a bitch, I hate life.

Saturday, April 17

Joe phoned and apologized for his behavior last night. He stuttered so about it, tho, that it is probably just as bad as before. Anyway, I know that I never want to see a HILL boy as long as I live.

---

44 It's not clear in this entry if this was her brother or another boy named Joe. The phone call afterwards indicates that it was probably not her brother, as he was still living at home at the time.

Van came down sick with small pocks [smallpox].[45] Now I'm exposed to them, so I guess I'll have to go get vaccinated.

I came out to Marjie's tonight. We're going horseback riding tomorrow.

Sunday, April 18

Gee, but I had fun today. We took our [riding] knickers in a suitcase to Sunday School and changed our clothes in the basement. Then we went down to the stables to get our horses. The stable boy hadn't brought our horses down from the pastures yet, tho. He said that we could go with him to get them if we would ride them back bareback. Of course we were willing, so we went with him. Had an awful time catching the horses but finally rounded Belle and Silver up. It was terribly bumpy riding back but fun. Then we saddled them and started out. We went clean down to Oswego[46] and fun! Say!! Our horses were just brimming with pep and ready to race *all* the time.

Once at Oswego I was trying to make him jump a ditch. A lot of people were watching, and it made me mad when he wouldn't jump. I was just about ready to give up when he reared way up on his hind legs and looked so wild and pretty. Of course, that made a sensation, so I was satisfied. I enjoy making a sensation!!

On the way home we were on a small country road, and I saw a rickety old Ford approaching. My horse was galloping at the time, and she made straight for the Ford. I wasn't very scared at first because I thought of course she would go around it. But the dumb animal would not be swerved from her course. She didn't stop until she was right square in front of it. The Ford stopped at the same time, and it was full of High School kids.

---

45 Smallpox had not yet been eradicated as a communicable disease and occasionally made an appearance in the West Coast's port cities. Some 1,235 Clackamas County school children were inoculated against smallpox in the first half of 1926.
46 Lake Oswego, about nine miles south of Portland.

One boy held his stomach and yelled, "Ouch!" He looked so cute. Black curly hair and real collegiate.

Oh, but I love to ride. To feel the wind whip back your hair and just dash madly along. Defying, challenging all to conquer. And I can gallop full speed with one hand in my pocket. Oh la-la. And tomorrow SCHOOL.

Monday, April 19

Didn't get home from Marjie's until this morning so didn't attend school. Mother says it was just an excuse to stay home. *Well,* maybe it was. What of it?

Tuesday, April 20

Went to school as usual. I got my report card today. I got B in English, C in Algebra, B in French, B in Phys [PE?], and A in Social Studies. I think that is pretty good. Daddy managed to restrain his joy, however. It's a tough life. These parents simply refuse to be pleased. The better I am, the better they want me to be.

Wednesday, April 21

Same old thing. Got up in morning, got dressed, grabbed some breakfast, and ran to catch the car. Almost missed it. Last to school, just in line for Chapel. Then Math, English, lunch, French, Science, and tennis. Then home again, study in the evening, write diary, then go to bed. Tomorrow I'll wake up and do the same thing. It's the darn monotony of it that I hate. I think I'll go mad.

I wish I could see Micky. I guess he has passed out of my life, tho. He was expelled from Lincoln and has gone to work. Joe doesn't know where he lives or anything. I guess he has just dropped out of my life. Darn it!! I want to see him. I wonder what he's doing and if he still looks the same. I think I love him!!!!!!!!!!!!!! Yes, I do, too!!!!!!!!!!!!!

Thursday, April 22

I played in the tennis tournament today with Bernice Congleton and lost by one point. Terribly discouraging. Oh well! That's better than not fighting at all. I got lots of compliments on the good fight I put up. Alyce has the mumps. Poor kid. She just phoned me. She had a keen date with Loren for tomorrow night, and now she can't keep it. She was nearly in tears, and I can't say that I blame her. The mumps is such a childish thing to get, too.

Friday, April 23

I stayed in for deficiency list tonight. Algebra as usual. It always was my worst subject. Went to show with Mother and Daddy. Saw Harold Lloyd in "For Heaven's Sakes."

Saturday, April 24

I went over to see Alyce today. Then met Marjie down town. We went to see "Beverly of Graustark." It was a wonderful picture. But between the end and the beginning, they had a lot of Pathe news. It was terribly boring. We were right up at the top of the balcony. Behind us was a door. When no one was watching, we went up there. Inside we found a ladder that led to the roof. Naturally we climbed up. It was lots of fun. Marjie is such a darn good sport. We're going to Mt. Hood tomorrow. Gee, I can hardly wait.

Sunday, April 25

We went to Mt. Hood today and hiked ten miles through three feet of snow. Lots of fun. Gee, but I love Marjie. Our chief occupation was giggling.

Monday, April 26

Hot day. I hate school.

Tuesday, April 27

Another hot day. Will this heat never end? Oh!! Today about five o'clock Al Baker came up and took me for a ride. He has a snappy line, but I don't think I like him. He's just a trifle *too* modern. Cute, tho, and popular, so I guess I should be flattered. He has pretty hair. I saw Mrs. Edwards on her back porch today placidly smoking a cigarette. *Umm!!*

Wednesday, April 28

Hot day. I can't decide who to ask to the Prom. I'd like to ask Micky, but I can't get him. Oh, how I love him. Then I suppose I could ask Jack Hibbard, but I'm supposed to be mad at him. I could ask Bill Whitely or maybe Hale. Heck!! I can't decide.

Thursday, April 29

Both Helen Dunn and Eveline want to take Bob Stryker to the Prom. I wanted Helen to take him, so I told Bob that she said for him not to forget that she was taking him. He said all right, he'd be willing to take her. This evening I phoned him to get Helen's phone number, and we got to talking about the dance. He said that he hated to go with either of the girls because that would make the other terribly mad at him. I asked him if he thought that Jack Hibbard would go with me. He said, "Oh, are you going?"

"Yes."

"Well, listen, you put in your bid for me and let me take you. Please, I'd rather take you anyway."

What should I have said? If I let him go with me, Helen would have a fit. Besides, I want Jack. I was flattered, tho. It was an awful temptation for me to say "yes," but I hated to disappoint Helen. She's so *very* crazy about him. So I said I'd think it over. Darn!! Why couldn't Jack be just as crazy to take me? Damn ——

I saw Bob Hibbard today. Gee! but he's adorable.

Friday, April 30

I can't decide who to take to the Prom. Darn it!! I'm tempted to take Bob [Stryker], but Helen likes him too well.

The view of downtown Portland from Luther R. Bailey's office in the Northwestern Bank Building, circa 1920.

Saturday, May 1

Met Eleanor down town today. Went to a show. I phoned Bob and told him that I put my bid in for him. He said, "Oh, have you, honest? Gee, I asked Helen." Of course I pulled the insulted guy [?], and he got awfully worried. He said, "Listen, Jack Hibbard will go with you."

"No, he won't. He goes too steadily with Marcine."

"Oh, but he doesn't. He likes you!!!!!!!!!!!!!!"

Sunday, May 2

Today while I was out in the Ford, Jack phoned. He said that he would phone later but didn't. Darn!! I don't know whether to ask him to come or not. Maybe he'll phone tomorrow.

Monday, May 3

Evaline said that Bob said that Jack told him that he didn't want to take me. But Bob said that he didn't say that. Who am I to believe? Evaline or Bob? If Jack would only phone me.

Tuesday, May 4

If Jack doesn't phone by tomorrow, I'm going to phone him!!!!!!! Elizabeth phoned tonight and wants me to go to a Progressive dinner Saturday night and dance afterward. I think I will. It will be fun and a good excuse to get a new dress.

Wednesday, May 5

I got the *cutest* new dress. I've never been so wild about just a dress in *all my life*.

Thursday, May 6

Why, oh, why, doesn't Jack phone? I think I'll ask Frenchy. I wish I could get in touch with Micky. He was expelled from school, and I can't reach him. I've *got* to see him.

Friday, May 7

Today I asked Micky's cousins if they knew where he was. They just glared at me and said for me never to speak his name in their presence as long as I lived. Gee, but I'm worried. Maybe they've put him in exile or something.

Saturday, May 8

Gee, but I had fun tonight. I went to that Progressive dinner. They had our partner all picked out for us. I had an awfully dumb dinner partner. After that we went back to the church. We lined up and marched around to meet our partners. I had John Goss. As we were standing in line, John Painton came up and said, "There's some mistake. Doris, you're my partner." I said, "How did that happen?" and he said, "Well, I got your name after a lot of trouble!" So I said I'd go with him.

Then we went out to get in the cars that took us to the dance, and in the scramble for the cars, I lost Johnny and got Remond Dunton. He was the cutest one of the bunch and had a darling car. We got four other kids and went out to Oswego instead of the Sunday School Party. Fun!! They knew their onions, too. We didn't get back until now, which is 12:30 [a.m.]. I'm hungry!!

Sunday, May 9

Went horseback riding today. We had a marvelous time and the most WONDERFUL horses. We took them to the beach and went swimming. The water was terribly cold. We were an hour late and used up all our money. The only thing we could do was start walking back. Seven miles. We hoped and prayed for a lift, and finally a one-eyed man in a rickety Ford came along. Of course we refused because he was so vulgar looking. In about half a mile he appeared again and wanted to know if we were tired walking. We said, "No." Pretty soon he came again and asked us. We had a terrible time getting rid of him. He asked us *five* times. Finally, two girls that Marjie knew came along, and we went with them.

Monday, May 10

Oh, Micky, darling, sweetheart, what have they forced you to do? Jack Caplan got a letter from him today, and the postmark was CHINA. He had run away, jumped aboard a lumber ship, and played stowaway. Now he scrubs floors on the deck of an old dirty steamer. Micky! Oh my own. There is so much good in him, and now he'll get tough and chew tobacco and get tattooed. Maybe I can't see him for 4 or 5 years. Maybe never!! Oh, Micky, write me please.

I can just see him in the cabin of a dirty boat. Getting kicked around and treated like a dog. All he gets to eat are hard biscuits and leftover stuff because he is at the lowest rank. I wonder what he is doing right now. Probably on his knees scrubbing the deck of an old ship. His black hair all rumpled and hanging over his forehead. The merry twinkle is absent from his cheerful blue eyes, and his firm mouth is firmer than ever. He is probably getting cuffed and receiving harsh words from older men. Many boys would not stick that out, but he will. His chin isn't determined and held high for nothing.

Soon they will realize that he is somebody, that he has character, and maybe, someday, he will be captain. But oh, Micky darling. You will have to go through so much, and you're so young and nice. You'll come face to face with things which you never have before. I know that you need me. I cried when Joe told me. I couldn't help it because you dared to face that all alone. Oh, you darling, adorable, please keep nice and clean and *don't* get tough.

Tuesday, May 11
I can't get my mind off Micky. I love him, I know I do. And I'm going to wait for him. It may be months, it may be years, but throughout everything I shall wait. Why, I'm just like a character in a book. Waiting through the years for my lover, and someday he shall come. Sometime he will realize that I am waiting and will come to me. We'll get married and live in a quiet little cottage by the ocean. I'd be content to live in a shack if I could be with him. Oh, the darling!

Maybe he thinks I would disapprove of his running away. If he would only write to me. I'm never going to kiss another boy. I'm going to have nothing more to do with them, because I've discovered the only one. He is my aim in life. I shall keep my lips fresh and clean for only him, and SOMEDAY he'll come back.

Wednesday, May 12
Dull day, nothing happening.

Thursday, May 13
Today while we were supposed to be having gym, a bunch of us girls were out under a tree by the fence. Jay Eccles and some other Lincoln boys drove up. We were leaning over the fence talking to them, and Sister Ellen Juliana came out and scared them away. We had a picnic at school today and danced afterward. It lasted until 7 o'clock. Were going to have the tennis finals but it rained. I hate school!!!

Doris and Rae, going out on the town.

Friday, May 14

Had the finals today. E. St. Clair walked off with the prize. Rae took me to see "The Student Prince." It was light opera. I didn't want to go very much because I thought it would be dry. It wasn't, tho. The singing was wonderful. The acting would have been good if he hadn't overdone it so. Just because he couldn't go to school, he raved and threw himself on the floor and sobbed. I thought it terribly exaggerated, but everyone clapped a lot, and Rae said that they were always dramatic at an opera. Then it ended wrong. He married the one he didn't want to. I prefer movies!!!

Saturday, May 15

Met Alyce down town today and went to a show. *Van phoned.* Maybe I'll take him to the Prom if he turns out all right. He was coming over tomorrow, but Mill Rawlings is coming from Seattle. He hasn't seen me since I was fourteen and didn't powder my nose. I want to spend my time in vamping him.

I'm worried about the exams.

Sunday, May 16

Well, well, well! Today Alyce and Loren came up. We got in his car and went below the hill. We were just driving past HMA when Jack Hibbard came out. I had meant to be cold to him, but he looked too cute. He got in the back seat with me, and we drove out to Oswego. At first I was in one corner and he was in the other. He got closer and closer. Finally he put his arms around me, kissed me, and said, "Let's make up." Of course he was irresistible as usual, so I leaned against him. We then had a hot necking party for 10 miles.

Then we got some canoes. Jack wouldn't sit with Alyce even when she begged him. Gee, but I got a kick out of that. It began to rain, so we launched the canoe under some trees. Loren and Alyce got out, and Jack pushed off. We had a gay 15 min[utes], just we two, and then came back after them. Gee, but Alyce was mad, and Loren madder. On the way back, the rain came down in TORRENTS. We were drenched by the time we reached the float. Of course Jack kept me warm on the way back in the car, and—oh boy—Alyce kept looking back at us at critical moments. So Jack said, "Hell, but I'd give a lot to spank you." Then he grabbed her, pulled her over the seat and Loren walloped her. After that the boys nearly died with laughter.

Jack sang romantic songs all the way home, and oh, but I'm happy. I can't wait to tell Marcine and Ruth. I think I'll take him to the Prom. He asked me to. I don't like his nose, but he has marvelous eyes. He was terribly flattering today, too. Gee, but I like him!!! He wanted to pet, but I didn't let him. Mugging is enough for me. Maybe I'm old-fashioned, but "what do I care?"[47]

He wanted a date!!!!!

But the way he kisses—when I think of his cool firm lips pressed tightly against mine, his arms drawing me closer, closer, and closer, I feel a funny prickly sensation in my spine. He is so strong, masterful, and mannish. Yet he is gay and a good sport.

Especially on the way home, when he was singing to me. Soft melodious music. Then it was that I felt happy. I felt as if I could ride forever and ever with his arm encircling me. It's funny, most boys aren't that thrilling. He is the only one besides Micky that *thrills* me.

And tomorrow school!!!

---

[47] "What Do I Care?" was recorded Jan. 5, 1926, by the International Novelty Orchestra; composer Sigmund Romberg, lyrics by Harry B. Smith. It's listed as a "medley fox trot" on the record label (Victor).

Monday, May 17

Study, study, study. Gee, but I hate school.

Tuesday, May 18

Hot day. I think I'll take Volmar to the Prom.

Wednesday, May 19

I put my bid in for Volmar. Now if he doesn't take me, I will be in dutch. Only one more day of school, then exams, then FREEDOM. HOT DOG!!!!

Gee, I hope I pass the exams.

Monday, May 24

I've been study and working for exams, haven't time to write.

Tuesday, May 25

I took French and Sacred Study exams today. Oh, but they were *awful*.

Wednesday, May 26

Math exam tomorrow. Oh! But I hope I pass it. Then Commencement and then—The Double O.[48]

Volmar phoned me up late this afternoon. He thinks he can get Gordon Penney's coupé to take us to the Prom in. Gee, won't that be great? I am anxious to see what he is like when you get out with him.

---

48 The Double-O Ranch (founded 1875) was one of the first permanent pioneer settlements in the area. William "Bill" Hanley, who owned the Double-O Ranch at the time of this diary, had made the ranch a retreat for guests.

Thursday, May 27
Uneventful day.

Friday, May 28
Oh Damn!! Alyce came over to stay all night. We didn't have anything to do, so we went to the show below the hill. We sat in the balcony, and a couple of Hill boys saw us and came over to sit with us. We were having a good time, and we heard a commotion behind us. We turned around, and it was Jack H. and another boy. Jack said, "Say, Doris, what did you tell Marcine that I said about her?"

"Why, nothing, except that you said that she smoked."

"Well, I wish you would keep your mouth shut. Now Marcine is off of me."

"Why, Jack, I didn't know I shouldn't tell her. I'm sorry, I didn't think."

"That's not all you told her. She wouldn't say what else. Now she's off of me. You must have made up some damn lie. I wish you would keep your mouth shut. You poke your nose into other people's affairs and don't think. Now Marcine hates me and blah blah blah."

I've never had a boy speak to me like that before. Especially him. I tried to apologize, but he wouldn't let me. And he looked so mad. It hurt my feelings terribly, so I turned around and shut my eyes tight to keep the tears from rolling down.

A cold realization was dawning. Marcine was jealous and had made up something so that Jack wouldn't like me. I should have gotten mad, but I just sat there dumbfounded. Didn't even deny it, just let him think I *had* said something. I became so sorry for myself that I was about to cry, so I decided to laugh and act as if nothing had happened. But I kept seeing

91

his eyes, steely gray, and heard his biting words in my ears. I've never been so miserable in all my life. Finally the show was over, and Jack walked out with us. He took his post beside Alyce and proposed to walk home with us.

While we were walking up those long steps, Eddie and me stopped at a landing to rest. He put his arm around me, and I had held back my tears so long that I had to give in. I put my head on his shoulder and wept tears of salt, meanwhile pouring out my heart to him. He spoke soothing words, and I felt better. When we got home, I invited them in, and Jack came. After he had called me all sorts of names, he had the nerve to accept my hospitality. I was so mad.

We made coffee and toast and ignored each other. Once when I was drinking my coffee, our eyes met over the cups. We just stared at each other for a full second. Finally he left. *Oh, how I hate him, despise him.*

I hope Marcine is satisfied—she has broken up one of the best friendships I ever had. DAMN.

Saturday, May 29
Went to a show with Alyce.

Sunday, May 30
Dull day.

**Rae (left) and friends at Council Crest in front
of the roller coaster, May 18, 1918.**

Monday, May 31

I've had a wonderful day. Alyce, Fanny, and I went to Council Crest[49] this afternoon. We saw Perry, Lloyd, and Bob Brandon. Lloyd and Bob went on the Blue Streak with us. Perry—well, you can guess the rest. Gee, but I *hate* him.

Tonight of course was the Junior Prom. Van came up and got me in his brother's car. His brother took the car when we got there and went on a date of his own. I had a wonderful program[50] and met some of the *cutest* boys. Good dancers, too. Helen brought a boy named Fritze. His name at first attracted me, and so I danced with him. Oh! After that we had five

---

[49] An amusement park located at Council Crest, a hilltop park, from 1907 to 1929. The Blue Streak was a roller coaster.

[50] She means that her dance card had many names on it—boys asked for a certain dance, and she wrote it in her dance program. They would get together for that dance.

dances, and then we were asked to give a feature dance. Gee, but it was fun. And the best part of it was that Jack was there, and I snubbed him cold.

He looked awfully cute and I didn't want to ignore him, but when I saw him lingering so near Marcine, I had to. Oh, I hate her. And she had that satisfied grin of possession on her face. She knows that through a lot of lying she has him for good now. Damn!

Anyway, I didn't let that spoil my evening. I got my share of attention from the other boys, so I was satisfied. Mr. and Mrs. Hall came for us. Bob, Eveline, Van, and myself sat in the back seat. Van put his arm around me, and we were whizzing along when all of a sudden the car stopped short. There was a crash of breaking glass, a scream and I bumped my head. We had hit a street car and were perched right on top of the cow catcher.[51]

We climbed out, and I was so disappointed to find that I wasn't even cut. After a whole crowd of people had gathered, they pushed the street car away. It seemed as if the whole side of our car would be smashed, but it wasn't even dented. And the street car: two broken doors, three broken windows, and the whole front pushed in. Gee, it was funny.

We stood around for about an hour, Mr. Hall doing a lot of arguing. Finally we got in the car and started home. Just as we turned up Culpepper, Van kissed me. Gee, but it was thrilling. He was so masterful and strong. Altogether it's been what I call a perfect day. I love a wreck.

Tuesday, June 1
What do you know about that? Here it is the first of June. I'm all through with school and freedom is mine.

---

51 The metal grille or frame projecting from the front of a train engine that serves to clear the track of obstructions (such as cows).

We had commencement tonight. Gee, but it was pretty. We all marched in our white veils and white dresses. I felt so sanctified. Of course there was a lot of ceremony, and Bishop [Sumner] preached a wonderful talk on Youth. I was so inspired. When we marched out of the church, the HMA boys were all lined up double file with their guns over their shoulders. We passed right between them. I felt just like a nun.

Wednesday, June 2
Came out to Marjie's today. We went down to the beach and fooled around. Mr. Mead said he would take us to Eastern Oregon next Monday or Tuesday. Just think, won't it be wonderful? Tomorrow Marjie and I are going to approach our daddies for new knickers, riding boots, and sombreros. I hope we succeed.

Thursday, June 3
Marjie and I went down town and ate lunch with Daddy. I think maybe he will let me have new knickers and a sombrero. Gee, but I hope I can. It was terribly hot down town. On the way home we both got boy hair-cuts for Eastern Oregon. I think I like them, and they'll be so convenient to go horse back riding in. After dinner we went for a boat ride down to the beach and talked O-O over with Mr. Mead.

Friday, June 4
Went down to the beach today. Ned was there. Gee, but Marjie is lucky to have him like her so well. I wish someone was crazy about me. I asked Walt why Fridze never came down anymore and he said that Fridze was working. Darn. After dinner Marjie and I wanted to go down to the beach because there was going to be a gang down there and maybe Fridze. They wouldn't let us, tho.

Saturday, June 5

Went down to beach. I wish Fridze would come down once in a while. It would be more exciting. After dinner Marjie and I rowed down to the beach. We talked to Mr. Mead about definite plans of the trip. We're leaving next Thursday. Gee, I can *hardly* wait. He's awfully nice to take us down there, I think.

Coming back about 9:30 the river was so pretty, so dark and mysterious. And the trees were so stately and majestic along the bank. Then the old mill silhouetted against the sky looked so romantic. Gee, I love Marjie.

I kept thinking of Micky today. I think my love for him is such a sacred thing. I know that someday he will come back to me, and oh, how I like him.

Sunday, June 6

We went to Columbia Beach[52] today. It was terribly hot and windy. Lots of common people there. We got back about 6:30, so Marjie and I went down to the beach. The water felt so good and cool. There were lots of tough boys there that tried to get us to go canoeing with them, but we didn't do it. About dark, one of the boys got a phonograph out on the float, and we danced. It was fun. When it was *real* dark, we tied about 6 canoes on the back of Mr. Mead's motor boat, and he towed us way up past Milwaukie. Fun!! There is a boy there that I rather like. His name is Darnel.

Monday, June 7

Went down to beach today. Had a pretty good time. Ned seemed to think it was his duty to push us in and get my hair straight. We had some canoe battles, and once when the canoe tipped, I scratched my ankle. That's about all the excitement we had. Oh, boy, this time next week I'll be in Eastern Oregon. Galloping across the desert on a wild mustang. Oh.

---

52 Columbia Beach opened in 1915; it was about seven miles north of Portland.

Tuesday, June 8

Went to beach today. It was rather cold, so we didn't stay in long but got dressed about 4 o'clock. Marjie and I went up in the launch to get a log to bring down to the float to play on. Mr. Mead tied it on to the back of the boat, and of course we were assailed with the bright idea to ride it. We had overalls on, and it was a foolish thing to do. Anyway, we did it.

The log rolled eventually, and I fell in with a horrible sensation. The water oozed around and about me. Gee, it was awful. I couldn't hardly swim because my shoes were so heavy. When we got back to the float, Ned, Walt, and Jack all told me how funny I looked. Of course that made me feel awfully good. I like them, tho. They're such a good-natured bunch.

**It was not unusual in the lumber-industry areas around
Portland for kids to play on logs in the waterways.**

Wednesday, June 9

We're going to Eastern Oregon tomorrow. Oh—I can hardly wait, I'm so excited.

Thursday, June 10

We left at 3 o'clock this morning and rode and rode and rode. We came up the McKenzie Pass[53] and are camped at Suttle Lake.[54] Gee, but it's pretty. I just took a dip in it and was the first one in. Umm. Gee, I'm happy.

Friday, June 11

We left early this morning for the O-O. We came through 180 miles of desert sagebrush. Gee, but it was pretty. Just like Zane Gray's descriptions. Hot. We ate lunch at the halfway house and finally got here. Oh, but it's pretty.

It's nestled among lots of trees, and behind it rises as if for protection a large rim rock. Then there is the bunk house, the feed house, and lots of corrals. Just an ideal ranch and some cowboys. One is especially cute. There is a dance in the valley tomorrow night. Maybe we can go.

Saturday, June 12

Marjie and I went for a horseback ride this morning. Way across the desert. When we came back, the cowboys were shearing sheep, so we went in to watch them. We soon made friends, and they said, jokingly, "Wouldn't you like to shear them?" We took them up on it and sheared half a sheep. Fun!

After dinner we went to the corrals again, and they were stomping wool. We had lots of fun, and Jess is *so* cute. Black curly hair, big brown eyes, and he talks Texas-y. Marjie left after a while to catch a kitten, and we

---

53 Now Old McKenzie Pass, Highway 242, east of Eugene, in the Willamette National Forest.
54 About 150 miles southeast of Portland.

were alone. We talked and talked. He taught me to roll a cigarette and everything. Oh, but he's cute.

I love the ranch *so* much.

Sunday, June 13

Marjie and I went to visit Old Chapel [Chapo] today. She's a Mexican woman and is half crazy. She lives all alone with her cats and dogs. Gee, but she is an interesting character. It was a long ride, about 12 miles over the desert and fun, too! Jess was cold today. I don't think he likes me very well.

Monday, June 14

Marjie and I went out to wrangle our own horses today because Ed was busy shearing sheep. We didn't have any horses to wrangle with so had to walk. I walked way around and almost got them when they pranced across a small lake. Then I had to go way around again and would almost get them and they'd bound off again. Oh, but I was mad. Somehow I got stranded across a little stream, and I was too tired to go around, so I just stood there. Then I saw Ed's beautiful horse come into view. As he drew nearer, I saw that Jess was on him. He came up and said, "Why, you poor little kid!!" Then he waded across the stream, and I climbed on his horse. We shooed the horses in and went back to the corrals. Alas, that ride was all too short.

He talks *so* cute. Says *hoss, good mawnin, hea*, and everything like that. And his eyes—oh.

When we finally got started, Marjie and I went way over a mountain and down a long canyon. We got right down in the center, and it seemed as if there was no human life for miles around. We saw a coyote and *lots* of rabbits. Then we climbed high upon the top of the world. The canyon was beautiful, but it seemed dark and sinister compared to the burst of glory that greeted us at the top. Then we took a short cut down the mountain again to the valley. We didn't realize that it was so steep until we were halfway down. Then it was too late to turn back. Oh, but it was *awful*. The hill was almost perpendicular. We led our horses down, of course, but my horse kept stumbling, and I was afraid he would fall on top of me. Gee, but it was scary. I got *sick* at my stomach before the bottom was reached.

There is a man that killed a man in the room next to us. We're scared he might go crazy and murder us all.

Tuesday, June 15
We had another pretty horseback ride today. When we came back, they were branding a couple of colts. Marjie and I sat on the fence and watched them. Jess would get on his horse, swing his lasso around and around, and rope a little colt. Gee, but he looked cute. It was mean, tho, the way they branded them.

After dinner Marjie and I went out in the cook house and talked to Jess, Ed, and Winnie. Fun. Marjie likes Jess too well to suit me. She's getting terribly conceited.

Wednesday, June 16
Marjie and I went Buckarooing today. We left at 9 o'clock and rode over desert lake bottoms, hills, and prairies. When we would see a tribe of horses, we would dash madly after them, and our horses would snort and throw their heads up high. Sometimes Jess would lasso them and everything. Then we would ride for miles and miles before we would see another tribe. Gee, but it was thrilling. We didn't get home until 7 tonight. Just think!! Ten hours in the saddle. I'm terribly tired, too.

It got so hot out on the desert, but I'm going again tomorrow. My face is sunburned, and I look TERRIBLE.

Yesterday when everyone was away, I yielded to temptation and went into the bunk house. I was so overcome by curiosity to see what the place Jess slept in looked like. I enjoyed exploring it. Last night I missed my hat and thought one of the dogs had taken it, so I told everyone to look out for it. This morning Ed found it in the bunk house and gave it to me.

I said, "Oh, one of the dogs must have taken it in there" and walked away. It's possible to get away with anything with old red-faced Ed. But this afternoon when there was a lull in the conversation, Jess said, "Say, how did your hat get in the bunk house?"

"Why, I guess Snoozer dragged it in."

"Yes, and hung it on a chair."

I was caught. I realized that, so I said, "I guess I might as well confess. My curiosity got the better of me, and I yielded to temptation to explore it. I've been so curious to see what it was like."

I was scared all the time I was talking for fear that he would be mad. Then I looked at him, tho he only grinned and his eyes twinkled like stars. Gee, but he's cute.

Thursday, June 17
Marjie and I curried our horses today. Then we rode them down to the lake and washed them. Billy Taylor is so slick and shiny now. Gee, but I love him. Hot dog.

Jess left today for the Bell A Ranch.[55] I'll miss him.

---

55 Another Hanley ranch, three miles east of Burns, Oregon.

Friday, June 18

The other day when we went Buccarooing [*sic*], Ed's horse got crippled. He had to turn him loose in the field because he was too crippled to walk home. Today a bunch of us went out to look for him, but we couldn't find him. They are afraid he might be dead. Gee, but I hope not.

Saturday, June 19

We looked nearly all day for Ed's horse. They think that he isn't able to reach water and is dead.

Martha has gone to Burns, so we ate at the cookhouse today. Gee, but I like it. It's so jolly and nice. I like Winnie, too. She told us all Jess's history.

**Doris (left) and Marjie (facing camera)
pose in their riding duds, circa 1928.**

Sunday, June 20
Today they all gave up finding Joe [the horse]. Said that he must be dead. But Marjie, me, and Helen all went out to look for him and *found* him. My, but we felt triumphant. He *was* almost dead, but we led him back to the ranch, and we're going to take care of him.

After dinner Marjie, Helen, and I took a long horseback ride. We found an old deserted house way down in a canyon and explored it. When we came back, we told the boys about what a nice dance hall it would make. They nearly went into spasms. Said that the house is haunted. An old Indian had murdered his wife there, and her ghost haunted the house. They even said that they had *seen* the ghost. Of course Marjie and I wanted to saddle our horses and go up there tonight. But Martha wouldn't let us. *Oh*, but we were mad. Then the boys laughed and said that we were afraid to go. And we couldn't prove that we weren't. They said that nothing could drag *them* up there.

I think of Micky constantly.

Monday, June 21
It was terribly hot today. Marjie and I washed all our clothes. Just about lunchtime someone yelled FIRE!! Of course we all dashed out there, and the corrals were all ablaze. We carried water from the pump to the fire and back again in the blazing hot sun. The cows mooed and made a terrible fuss. We finally put it out, tho.

Bill is rather cute. Kind of insipid, but I like him. I like the whole ranch, for that matter. It's friendly and nice. I wish Jess were here. Marjie and I giggle *constantly*. Honestly, it's almost embarrassing. We got started today at the table and couldn't stop. Gee, but it was awful.

Tuesday, June 22

I've never lived through such a hot day. I didn't even feel in the mood to go riding. This evening we had fun, tho. Marjie and I went over to the cookhouse and danced and acted generally silly. Martha said that if we giggled much more at the table, she would make one of us stay at the cookhouse. It is awful. Why, we go into perfect spasms over nothing at all.

Wednesday, June 23

Say, talk about your *hot* days!! It was up to 112 in the sun, 106 in the shade. Just imagine!! Marjie and I were struck with the bright idea to go swimming. We put on our bathing suits and rode our horses [a]long back down to the dam. It came to our *knees*, and when we tried to swim, we would find ourselves floundering in a bed of gooey mud. We came home and got two big tubs of water. Put them just outside our door and sat in them. With nothing on. *Fun!!*

This evening we rode our horses out toward the sunset. Gee, but it was pretty. I wish Micky were here, but I love Marjie *so*. Martha is getting kind of cranky. She said that we stewed around and caused a lot of trouble. Kind of a funny thing for a *hostess* to say.

Thursday, June 24

Oh, boy, was it hot today. 105 in the shade at 10 o'clock this morning. It climbed to 115 later in the day. We made ice cream and loafed around. Tonight there was a small thunder storm, but it didn't amount to much.

Friday, June 25

Another hot day!!! Marjie and I got tubs of cold water, sat in them with our sombreros, and read our books. Tonight we went to the haunted house. We left about 7:30, and the moon hadn't come up yet. Just as we came on top of the ridge, it came out in all its glory. I've never seen such a red moon in all my life.

We laughed and talked gaily enough at first, but towards 9 o'clock, when it had become dark and we were entering Rattlesnake Gulch, something subdued our spirits. I can't explain it. I don't think it was fear because there was really nothing to be afraid of. But I felt tense, and my hands were clenched over the saddle horn. That darn gulch is so mysterious and forbidding with all its caves and bleached bones. As our horses walked over the bones, they made an awful crunching sound.

Finally we came out of that terrible place and were walking in the general direction of the house. We couldn't see it yet because it was so dark. In fact, the only things in the world seemed to be us, the never-ending sagebrush, and a big red moon. And it was *so* quiet. Not even the buzz of a mosquito to break the death-like stillness.

Then out of the darkness loomed the house, dark, sinister, and uncanny. I had to *force* myself to ride up to the house. All of the stories I had heard about the Indian's ghost and blah, blah came back to me. My mouth felt dry, and my hand trembled as I *made* myself touch the outside of the house. Scared? Of course we were scared, and anyone would be. We started away at a gallop, but I couldn't resist looking back. I saw something white and waving standing in the window. Of *course* it was mostly my imagination plus a little bit of moonlight, but I didn't like it.

And then, to cap the climax, a coyote let out a long, drawn-out howl. Like the nuts we were, we lost the road, and rode for an interminable length of time through sagebrush. I was sure we were going to be lost in that death valley, but finally before us gleamed the road. Oh, but it was a welcome sight.

We were so happy that we began to sing and kept it up until, just directly in front of us, we heard a warning. A death warning that even the bravest of cowboys will not ignore. And that is the rattle of a rattlesnake. Believe me, we steered clear of it. Gave it a wide berth about a quarter of a mile. Gee, but the O-O looked good to us when we finally reached it alive.

Saturday, June 26
The thermometer was 100 *in the shade* today!!

Sunday, June 27
Well!! Uncle Will came today. This evening Marjie and I went for a ride. We met the Goldins, and they told us to get some old cows up in the Dun-field. I picked on an old black one and had an *awful* time. I had to chase her all over creation and soon lost sight of Marjie. Before I realized it, it was dark, and I got *so* mad at that darn cow. I've never wanted to *kill* anything so badly in *all my life*. She'd be going nicely, then all of a sudden would turn the opposite way, and I'd have to chase her for about a mile. Then she would chase me for a while. Oh, but it was *awful* and so dark. I'd stumble and nearly fall, and oh, how I swore at her.

About 1 o'clock [in the morning] I saw lights. It was the ranch coming to find me. They thought I had been killed or something. Gee, but I was glad to see them.

Monday, June 28
I went to get the damned old cow today and did it. Tho it took us nearly all day.

Tuesday, June 29
We went to see old lady Chapo today. She cried because she said she was so lonesome. Got terribly dramatic, too, and waved her arms around. Said that she had a heart as big as this whole universe. I almost cried, I was so sorry for her.

Wednesday, June 30

Talk about *sultry* days. Oh!! I rather like Bill. He's terribly bashful, and it's easy to fluster him and make him blush. He's kind of cute-looking, too.

Thursday, July 1

Forgot to write.

Friday, July 2

We're going to Burns[56] tomorrow. Hot dog!!

Saturday, July 3

We left ~~early~~ this morning and reached Burns about noon. Went to a show and monkeyed around. It certainly is a typical country town. Cowboys riding up and down the street and trying to flirt. Gee, but I liked it. This evening we went to a *prize-fight*, and talk about thrills. I've never been so excited before. Just to see them trying to kill each other. They got all bloody and everything. I yelled till I was hoarse. Lots worse than a foot ball game. Hal Hibbard won. He was the cutest boy, too, and it was so thrilling to see him clench his teeth and go after that man.

After the fight we went to the dance. Oh, but I had *fun*. I met some cute boys, too. I especially liked one of them, but I don't know his name. Marjie and I call him Freckles. He was awfully flattering and had pretty blue eyes. Some of them were *terribly* drunk. And one kept telling me he loved me. I like Milton, too, but he's rather old-fashion. He bought me some punch, tho, so I shouldn't kick.

I danced every dance and had to refuse lot of them. ~~Three~~ Five boys wanted to take me home. All this sounds conceited, but it isn't. I *did* have *such*

---

[56] Burns, Oregon, was the nearest town to the ranch, some forty miles to the northeast.

a good time. And *a whole* bunch said they were coming out to the ranch. Whoopee!! We're staying at Martha's brother's house tonight.

Monday, July 5

Oh!!!!!! I'll start at the beginning. Yesterday morning we had breakfast down town. Then after that we left for "Black Butte."[57] Isn't that a sinister sounding name? We didn't get there until evening. It's kind of a campground with tents and a platform in the middle of everything. All this is way off in the mountains. About 7:30 they started dancing, and we started, too. Martha said that we had to leave about 9 so to make the best of it. When 9 came, we didn't want to go so [we] persuaded her to stay until the end.

About 10 o'clock things began to liven up. I don't think I danced with a boy that wasn't half soaked. And some of them were saturated with liquor. It was a real Western dance. Cowboys and all, and everyone was so full of pep. Just brimming with it.

I met a cute boy named Ted Patterson. We called him Pat. And Marjie, one named Fulton. We four kind of stayed together. Both boys were marvelous dancers. Especially Fulton. Like the way he "fox trots." Oh boys!! They kept begging us to take a drink and blah blah. We didn't, tho. These boys were dressed nicer than the rest, too. Sporty sweaters and big pants. Pat had the remains, or maybe it was the beginning, of a mustache. It gave him such a Frenchy air. He was 26. Been married but divorced. Isn't that *nice*!! To have a married man fool around with you. He was flattering, too, and I like him.

Another good dancer I met at the Spring. Red headed. He whirled and dipped and said that I was the only girl that could follow him when he whirled. I had two or three with him. Then we began having "tag dances."

---

57 Black Butte is near Bend, about 130 miles west.

Oh, but *they* were fun, and I got tagged, too. I'd just start dancing with one, and I'd be switched to another. It seemed as if we had danced about three hours, and can you imagine my surprise when we saw the first red streaks of dawn peeping through the trees. We had danced *all* night long. After that we rode back to Burns and slept and slept and slept. Then we came to the O-O.

Tuesday, July 6

It rained and rained today. Mr. Goldin butchered a cow today. Gee, but it was awful. First he shot it, then he cut its neck, and the blood just spurted forth. Jess came home today.

Wednesday, July 7

Oh! We got mail from the folks today and have to go home!!! Leave the O-O. I can't bear to think of it. Damn!! I like Bob Hewitt. Also Pete, Jess, and Mustard plus Bill. Come to think of it, I like George Hewitt awfully well. He looks like Bob Hibbard. Mrs. Moon came. We've been eating at the cookhouse lately, and it's fun with all the cowboys and everything. There's a bunch of wild horses out in the corral.

I DON'T WANT TO GO HOME!

Thursday, July 8

I branded a horse today!! Gee, but it was fun. We also went swimming and visited the haunted house again. Tomorrow I have to go home!! Boo.

We are going to take the stage[58] and land in Bend [Oregon town] Friday night. Mr. Mead is going to meet us Sunday. That means two nights and seven meals. We only have 6 dollars between us. I don't see how we are

---

58 A bus-like service, possibly in a large car.

going to manage it myself. Maybe we'll have to camp. We can't afford a hotel.

Friday, July 9
We left the O-O this morning. Jess kissed me goodby in the corrals. Not bad—that.

Well!!! Here we are in the big sticks. Penniless in a big city. We caught the stage this morning. There was an adorable driver, so we sat in the front seat with him. When we got here, we looked all over town and finally found a funny little hotel (the cheapest in town). The rooms were 75 cents and $1.00. Of course we spoke for the 75 cent one, but when he took us up to look at it. Oh! Why, it didn't even have a window. Just a sky-light.

Then the man said he'd give us an outside room for 75 cents. Whoopee!! It's bad enough, kind of dingy, but better than nothing. We only have $1.00 left for meals. This is Friday night, and we have to last until Sunday. That gives us only 4 25-cent meals. That means we go without Sunday dinner. Oh, well, such is life! And we're having fun. It's kind of thrilling. *Gee whiz!!* But I'm hot. Only one little window, and it opens on an alley. Anyway, we're free to do what we darn well please.

The bed looks hard, and yet I'm sleepy, so I guess I'll turn in.

Saturday, July 10
Oh boy! The bed *was* hard. We got up this morning and had our breakfast of applesauce, toast, and milk, which cost 30 cents. That was more than we expected. About noon we started out for lunch. As we were crossing the street, who should drive by but Marie Hanes. She took us for a nice long ride and treated us to a milk-shake. We decided to let that be our lunch so that we would save some money. She also asked us to the dance. She said that Evaline had been going out with *Van*.

This evening Marie called for us, and we went to her friend's house. We tasted some whiskey, and it was *awful*. Then we went to the dance. Marie didn't like it, so went home. We stayed and had fun. Met two boys, and they took us for a ride after the dance. Of course we shouldn't have done it, but we did. We drove up to Pilot Butte.[59] Petted to a certain extent and smoked. He was terribly disgusting. When he kissed me, he spread his lips all over my face. Oh, but it was awful. It's now 3 o'clock.

Sunday, July 11
We went to church this morning on an empty stomach. Bought some bread and stole some butter from a restaurant. We put the butter in a glass of water to keep it cool. About 2 o'clock [the] Meads hadn't come, and we were getting desperate. We strolled down to the lobby. On the wall we saw a sign: "All those not checked out by 11 a.m. will be charged for another day." Oh, but we were scared.

We went up to our room, sat on the bed, and stared at each other. Then someone knocked on the door. We thought that we were going to get kicked out, and I said, "Come in," in a weak voice. The door opened and it was Mrs. Mead.

Oh!! We flew into her arms, and she brought us home tonight. We're at [the] Danas' now, and I'm going home tomorrow.

Monday, July 12
Home at last.

---

59 An extinct volcano near Bend.

My Diary

Beginning July 17
Ending September 14

No Tresspassing —
Private
Dangerous to Men and Etc.
No Parking
Do not Read
in other words —

Mind Your Own Business ! ! ! ! !

Love is Life
Life is Love

Saturday, July 17

Well, another new book. I used up the other one in *four* months. I hope this lasts longer. I went down town with Fanny today. We just hammered around. Not doing much of anything. When we were waiting at Bernie's for a street car, a couple of cute boys passed by in a car. They smiled, and we did like wise. Accordingly, they went around the block and came back. They did that *four* times. The fourth time, just as they were passing, they glanced back at us. Not looking where they were going, they naturally ran into another car. We got a big kick out of that. To think that *we* were the cause of a *wreck*.

We went to a show tonight. Not so bad.

Sunday, July 18

I drove the Ford over to Marjie's, and we went for a ride. Daddy said I could use it when I had an errand to do. Not bad—that. I wish something *exciting* would happen. This dull life is getting on my nerves. I want my *darling, sweet, adorable MICKY* for the plain and simple reason that I love him!!!!!!

Monday, July 19

I played tennis with Fanny this morning all morning. Met some cute boys up at the courts. Came home. Ate lunch. Took the Ford and drove down town and bumped into a car. Did something to the carburetor. Came home and got Joe. Took him around paper route. Ford baulked [*sic*] on hill and wouldn't come up, so had to resort to street car. Much to the conductor's amusement. Ate dinner. Read. And *that* constitutes the day's excitement. *Damn!!* I'm beginning to rebel. I crave adventures. I want to *live*. Not merely exist.

**Rae washes the family car—a Scripps-Booth—in this photo.
The Bailey children were able to drive at age sixteen.**

Tuesday, July 20

Went to a show with Fanny. We got something to eat afterward at Beck's. There was an adorable man in there that waited on us. Came over to Alyce's after dinner and am spending the night.

Wednesday, July 21

Alyce and I came over [to] town and went to a show. I never laughed so hard in all my life. The show was so darn funny. After that we went to Beck's. I wanted to see that man again. I did, too. Gee, but he's darling. Then I came home. After dinner I went up to Fanny's to play tennis. About 8 o'clock we came home. The folks were away, so we took the Ford and went down town. A couple of men followed us all over. They asked us to take a ride in a *good* car and blah blah. We had an awful time getting rid of them.

It's kind of funny that two girls can't go riding without being pestered to death. We got some gas at a cute service station. I'm going there after this. College boys were working there. Not bad—that.

Thursday, July 22
Took the Ford down to the Garage this morning and got tire fixed. After lunch, Fanny, Judy, the Ford, and I went to a couple of shows. After that we took Joe on his paper route and oh boy!!! We had just heaps of fun.

One time we stopped in front of an apartment, and two perfectly adorable boys asked us to come in. When we wouldn't do it, they came out. Two or three cars followed us and everything. This evening we took the car out again and stopped at a Drug Store for a Sundae. There was the most English Englishman I've ever seen who waited on us. He was cute, too. I'm staying all night at Fannie's.

Friday, July 23
My, but today has been a busy day. We got up this morning and went for a ride. In the Ford, of course. We played tennis a while and both ate lunch at my house. After lunch we went down and got a girl from the East who is visiting Mrs. McWaters and took her to a show. She was terribly dumb, and we were bored to death. We hurried her home and went for another ride ourselves. Then we came home and ate dinner.

After dinner we took the car out *again*. A cute boy followed us in a Ford Roadster. We let him catch up with us. He had red hair—red mustache and beautiful blue eyes. Fanny fell flat for him. He *was* rather cute, but I doubt if I could ever fall in love with a boy like that. He was too sophisticated looking.

Well anyway, she raved and raved about him. About that time we were feeling very much in need of some gas. We stopped at our service station, and there was the *cutest* boy there. He had light curly hair, big blue eyes, a dimple and a boyish laughing face. Of course I fell in love with him. He is the man of my dreams!!!

Saturday, July 24
Played tennis this morning with F.T. After lunch we took the car and went to a show. Fanny got her hair curled, and we got something to drink at Beck's. That cute man was there, and we had fun. Came home. Ate dinner and played tennis in the evening. Guess I'll go to bed!!

Sunday, July 25
I hate Sundays!!

Monday, July 26
Met Marjie D. down town this afternoon. We saw the *best* show. After that we went for a ride. I took her up to see my cute Service Station men, and they acted *so* cute. Then I took her to see my drug store boys. They were nice also. After that I took Marjie to her train and met Mother. We came home.

Then I took the car again and went to the library. Also to see Alyce but she wasn't home. I came by Ed's Service Station. He wanted a date. *Imagine* it!!!!!

Tuesday, July 27
Didn't do a darn thing all day long. I crave excitement. Fanny is leaving for British Columbia tomorrow. Wonder what I'll do with myself.

Wednesday, July 28

Gee, but today has been one hectic day. To begin with, I got up late, and the maid hadn't left me any breakfast. After lunch I went down town to do some shopping. After I had done it, I went to see if the car was finished. It wasn't, so I had to stand over the man until he finished. Then I started over to Alyce's. I had just crossed the bridge when I ran out of gas. Just about that time a middle-aged man drove up in a big car and asked me if I was having trouble (as if he couldn't tell that without asking). I said "Yes."

He asked me who I was, where I lived, and etc. He seemed to know Daddy. Anyway, he said "Since he was Southern, too,[60] he'd stake me to a gallon of gas," which he did. I thanked him profusely and started off once more, thankful that my troubles were so small.

About that time the engine began to bang and knock like a sledge hammer. I drove into a Service Station and asked the boy what in Hades was wrong with Billy Taylor.[61] He grinned and said, "Why, you've burnt out a berring[62] (what-ever *that* is). He very kindly called a Garage for me. The Garage man came. He also grinned, said that it would cost me five dollars and would take 2 or 3 hours to fix the D——— thing. Let him grin!!!

---

[60] Doris's parents were both Alabama natives.

[61] Her pet name refers to the car as well as the old English song "Billy Taylor."

[62] Bearing.

A car gets towed away after a wreck. Rae was on the spot with his camera.

I turned to the Service Station boy and said, "What will I do with myself for 2–3 hours?" And *he* with a *bigger grin* said, "Oh, you can use my coupe if you wish." Darling boy! I was beginning to like his grin. *So* I took his car before he changed his mind and drove over to Alyce's. I phoned Mother from there, and she gave me heck. Then we took the car and put some gas in it. Then went to Bib's.

Somehow we spent 3 hours here, there, and everywhere. About that time I decided to get my car. I went to the Garage, and the boy said, "Say, I've some sad news for you. The crank shaft is broken, and it will cost you *$37* and will take 3–4 *days* to fix it. ~~Imagine it!!!~~

"37 dollars!" I said and just stared at him. I had him call Daddy then; it was inevitable. He'd have to know sometime or other. The garage man explained it to him. Then Dad began to talk. We couldn't hear what he was saying, but it was evidently pretty tall language, because the perspiration began to break out on the man's face. After an interminable length of time, he hung up and said, "Say, if you ever put me up to another task like that, I'll die. I'm sorry for you if you have to go home."

I was afraid to go home, but I did. Took the long street car ride. Oh! But Daddy was *mad*. Said that I didn't know how to value money and etc. Ye gads! He acted as if I *wanted* that damned old crank shaft to break. And he was going to get us a roadster and now he won't. D——!!!!! And I *know* I'll never hear the last of it. Mother said that she was going to put me on 3 months' probation and blah, blah.

I went down to see about a job this evening. Couldn't get it, tho.

Thursday, July 29
I came out to Marjie's this afternoon, and we went swimming. Gee, but we had fun. It was so nice to just bask in the water. There was a big crowd, too, and lots of cute boys. Frankie was there. Gee, but I love Marjie.

Friday, July 30
Came home this morning and helped Mother all day. She's giving a dinner party, and oh, of all the noise. They talk about us kids making a racket, but I wish they could hear themselves. Oh ye gods!!!

Saturday, July 31
The usual fuss and wrangle about the Ford. There is now a bill of $75 on the damn thing, and I guess I'll never hear the last of it. Ye gods. I can't help it because the darn thing won't run. They won't even go to the beach tomorrow because of it. And I wanted to go so badly.

I met Alyce down town this afternoon. We fooled around and had something to eat at Beck's. Gee, but the man in there is a-dor-a-ble. He has a clever line, too. Alyce is going away tomorrow. Now I am the only one left in this fool town. Even Marjie is away. Went for a ride this evening over on the East Side. The new Hollywood Theater has just opened, and my, but it was jammed. Poor little Sandy Boulevard has so much traffic, it was dazed.

Sunday, August 1
Bob C. was visiting Joe all day. He took a sudden interest in me and wanted to take me for a ride. Fact which annoyed Joe very much. Brothers are such fools.

There were some people visiting from the East today. They hadn't seen me since I was about 6 years old. "Oh, how you've grown!" seemed to be all they could say. Of course I've grown since I was 6. I hope so, anyway.

Say! Guess who came to see me this afternoon? Billy Bader and John Maley, of all people. I nearly collapsed. We used to be childhood sweet hearts and all that sort of bull. Gee, but I was surprised to see him and glad, too.

Childhood sweethearts: Doris and Clayton M., a family friend, in July 1918.

Monday, August 2

We went to the Helie[63] tonight. It was pretty good as plays go. Kind of mystery-comedy. The actors did a lot of yelling and etc. to make the audience say it was good acting. What interested me most was a young couple who sat near us. Obviously madly in love with each other. They would look at each other with their souls in their eyes and so forth.

It made me realize how empty life is without my darling, sweet, adorable Micky. Oh, how I want him, long for him. I wonder if he'll come back to me? Alas! Only time will tell. But I feel sure that he will. I love him so.

Tuesday, August 3

Went down town for lack of any other excitement. Hot day.

Wednesday, August 4

Stayed home all day long. We were going to go to a show, but some fool people came to look at the house. They came about 7 and stayed too late for us to go. Some people simply do not know when to go home.

I wish I could find a job and get some money of my own. I hate to ask the family for money all the time. I'd like to be independent, and next summer will be different. I'll work!! And have some money once in a while.

Thursday, August 5

Went down town today and bought brassiere, bath salts, comb, manicure set, powder puff, and file.

---

63 The Heilig Theatre was a live theater venue that also presented motion pictures. Three years after Doris saw this show, Paramount Pictures took over and renamed the place The Rialto.

Jack Caplan got a letter from MICKY today. He is in Australia and plans to enter the interior with a group of 5 or 6 men, cross the desert, and dig up an old mine that is supposed to be rich. Oh, my Micky!! He said that he didn't know our address, so couldn't write to us, and he didn't have any definite address himself. Oh, Micky darling, will I *ever* see you again? He broke his arm on a ship, and I'll bet he suffered unendurable pain without a whimper. Believe me, I'd say more than that, but he wouldn't. Not my Micky. He's too brave. Oh how I *love him*.

Friday, August 6
Mother gave a luncheon today, and I had to serve. Bah!! My old Sunday School teacher was here, and I had to suffer her oh's and ah's. We went to a show this evening. Awfully good. It made me want my Micky. It seems as tho everyone is in love but me. That is—I'm in love without my lover.

Saturday, August 7
Hot day.

Sunday, August 8
I *hate* Sundays! I do, I do, I do. I haven't done anything exciting for ages. I'm being nearly bored to death. I wonder if people ever do die from boredom? I believe that it's possible.

Monday, August 9
I got a card from Marjie today. She's having a wonderful time and etc. Having a love affair and everything while I stay at home and read—BAH!!!

I went down town this afternoon. As I was coming up the elevator to Daddy's office,[64] Dick Detzi[e], Fred Yarnell's chum, got on the elevator.

---

[64] Luther Bailey had offices in the Northwestern Bank Building at 621 Morrison Street.

He smiled at me, an incident which surprised me muchly because he's never recognized me before. I've never given him much thought because he was usually with Fred, and naturally I have only eyes for him. Anyway, Fred wasn't with him, so it gave me a chance to study him. Clear up to the ninth floor. As I got off, I smiled at him and went my way. Later on, I went down to buy some stamps and came up again. As I got off the elevator, he came dashing around the corner and nearly bumped into me. He gave me the most dazzling smile and went on. He interests me!!

Damn! Oh Damn! Oh Damn—

It's nearly 12 [midnight], but I'm mad. About 10 o'clock Alyce and some boys drove by and honked for me. I got dressed and climbed down the balcony to see them. In about 10 minutes Daddy came out and said, "*Doris!* You come in the house!"

I said, "Just a minute, Daddy."

Pretty soon he came back and said, "*Mind me!* Come in."

Just *imagine* it. I was so mortified I nearly died. Then I invited them in the house, but they were afraid to come, and I don't blame them. It's awful, and everyone pities me because I have such cranky parents. When I finally *did* come in, Daddy raved and raved.

I'm sick of this.

The Northwestern Bank Building is where Luther R. Bailey kept his professional offices as an architect and real estate developer.

Tuesday, August 10

I went over to Alyce's, and we went to the Hollywood [Theatre]. She told me how popular she had been at camp and etc. Some people are *terribly* conceited.

Wednesday, August 11

I took Mother down town in the Ford today. On the way back I was alone, so went into the cute service station man's service station (oh ye gods!). He was perfectly adorable. Kept saying clever things, and as luck would have it, I was dumb! Couldn't think of a single clever remark. Just grinned at him. Even when he was being flattering, I blushed like a little school-girl instead of being cooly sophisticated. Oh death, where is thy sting?

After I had left there, I passed that Detzi[e] boy. He was in a Ford Roadster. He honked his horn and waved wildly. Of course I like people to know I know him, but he made me just a trifle too conspicuous, and I hate being made conspicuous. Oh well, such is life! ~~Just think of the sorrows, the happiness~~

As I sit here tonight, looking out at the brilliantly lighted city before me, I feel a calm descend upon my spirits. The city looks so prosperous and gay, so full of thriving humanity. It seems as if all the world must be happy. Still, maybe in that very group of lights, someone is suffering a terrible grief. Maybe poverty. The city undoubtedly seems cruel and hard to them. The lights are bright and glaring instead of cheery and welcome. It only stands for the things which they have been deprived of.

And possibly, a short distance from them, there is someone who is hilariously happy. They may not deserve the happiness a bit more than his neighbor, still, fate is so cruel and that is life. Ah, how much those lights hide. I wish I could pierce through them, see for myself the little plays enacted in this little bit of paradise. There are so many heroes that remain unsung, and so many thieves that remain unpunished.

I'm getting sentimental. Good night, dear diary.

Thursday, August 12

Well, they've actually consented to take me to Crater Lake.[65] I hope I have fun, tho I don't see much chance of it. Riding with two grown people and Jack [her younger brother]. They seem to think they're doing me a great favor, tho, so I'll have to be grateful. I could have had a date this weekend, too!!!

Anyway, we're going to Bend. And I know those boys. Maybe I'll have fun after all.

---

65 Crater Lake, Oregon, was formed when a volcano collapsed onto itself. The water is so clear because it is almost 100 percent snowmelt. It is about 250 miles from Portland, quite a drive in those days. Bend is 119 miles from the lake.

Friday, August 13

We left early this morning and rode all day long. In spite of the fact that it was Friday the 13th, we got here without mishap. My, all this sounds formal, but I feel that way. Sitting in a luxurious writing room to write my diary. It certainly is a contrast to the last time I stayed in a hotel. We're at Klamath Falls,[66] a cute, prosperous little mining town. It reminds me of a small Western village and of all the men! I'll bet three-quarters of the population are masculine. Young, too, and terribly inclined to flirt.

There was a cute one in the table next to ours in the dining room. Umm. We will be here until about noon tomorrow. Hope I have some fun. Then Crater Lake and then Bend.

I wish my curling iron would work.

**Oregon's Crater Lake, formed by an extinct
volcano, is a destination for sightseers.**

---

[66] Some sixty miles from the lake.

Saturday, August 14

Crater Lake! And oh, but it is beautiful. I don't blame the Indians for not wanting to give up this country. It's too beautiful to be true. This morning we took the trail down to the bottom. There were boys down there with boats that took us around the lake. A perfectly adorable boy was with us. He was about 20 or 21, Junior at U. of O.[67] He had black curly hair, pretty brown eyes. A cute mouth and a mustache that could be seen once in a while.

He talked to me most of the time, instead of telling the occupants of the boat the points of interest and etc. Made Mother rather mad, I think. Anyway, as soon as we landed, she hurried me away. In the evening, I went for a walk, and suddenly I heard a voice behind me. It was Bob, of course. He walked back to the hotel with me and flirted like heck with his pretty eyes. He said there was going to be a dance about 9 o'clock after the speech, and he asked me to go.

I said I would and was too happy to live. While they had the speech, he sat right in back of me, and I was thrilled to listen to the speaker. Silly, isn't it? Oh, I forgot to say, when he took us around the lake, he had on old clothes, but after dinner, oh! He had on white linen golf pants, white sweater, and loud sox [*sic*]. Too collegiate for words. After the speech I asked Mother if I could go to the dance and she said *no!!* Imagine it.

So I had to tell him I couldn't go. Of course he made a big fuss. Then he went on over to the dance floor. I fumed around, and finally Mother asked the manager about it. He said it was all right because he knew all the boys. They were nice lads and so forth. He introduced me to the bell-boy (from O.A.C.[68]), and he took me over. When I went in, I saw Bob standing over in the corner. Then we began to dance. I danced about five dances before Bob came over.

"May I have the next dance?" he said. As luck would have it, I already had it [booked], so had to give him the one after. He dances adorably and has

---

67 University of Oregon, in Eugene.
68 Oregon Agricultural College, at Corvallis, now Oregon State University, Corvallis.

the *cutest* line. I danced quite a few with him after that. I liked him because he didn't get so darned personal and suggestive. He was flattering without being vulgar. The nearest we got to being exciting was when I said, "Gee, my lips are chapped from that wind," [and] he said, "*Oh!!!*" significantly.

I said, "Oh, there isn't a chance for anything like that *around here.*"

"Oh, so you evidently don't think much of our boat boys."

I said, "Well, I don't really *know* them yet."

"~~Well,~~ you will, tho, if you stay too long. You're too tempting."

Just then as things were getting erotic, we were tagged, and I had to dance with a boy they called "The Major." But as I started to turn to him, Bob held my hand and gave it a thrilling little squeeze and an entrancing smile.

There was another boy there that attracted my interest. He was a guest at the hotel, and I overheard him telling someone that he had just graduated from O.A.C. He had black hair and a black mustache. *Very* English. He just stood in the doorway, tho, and didn't dance with anyone.

I mentioned the matter to one of the boys and asked him if he thought he was married. He was *so terribly* indifferent. "I'll bet he dances with *you*, tho, before he goes," the boy said.

I said, "Why?" and he said, "Well, everyone here has danced with you at *least* three times, and I doubt if he's an exception." I just laughed, but secretly hoped for the best. And sure enough, towards 11 o'clock, he sauntered over to Bob and me and asked for the next dance.

When we started away, I said, "Well, I thought you were going to ignore me all evening."

"I've had an awful headache," he said. "But thought I'd dance with you before I left. The others seemed to enjoy it so."

Wasn't that nice. For him to choose only poor little me in all that crowd. I liked him awfully well, and he wanted to take me back to the Inn, but I had to go with the other boy. One boy said, "Say, a fella has an awful time to get to dance with you. I never get there in time."

Oh! I forgot to say Bob dared me to ride the surf board tomorrow. No girl has ever done it, and I'm going to *do* it. I like Bob best, and when he comes to Portland, I may have a date. Whoopee!! When he found out I was leaving tomorrow, he said, "Oh, gee, why don't you stick around a while? I like you."

When we finally got back to the Inn, everyone had gone upstairs but the English man, and we stayed down and talked a while. Maybe it wasn't proper, but it was thrilling.

Sunday, August 15
Oh damn, damn, damn. Daddy insisted on leaving today right after breakfast, and I didn't get to ride on the surf board or say goodby to Bob or anything. The Bellboy was the only one, and he didn't count. I wanted to see my Bob.

I hope this isn't a romance that dies. I like him too well. The lake was beautiful this morning. Just a shimmering mass of blueness. We drove through some wonderful scenery, too, and nearly had some fatal accidents. Anyway, we're home and nothing to do.

Monday, August 16
Fanny came up today, and we fooled around. Nothing much to do.

Tuesday, August 17

I went down town this morning and had lunch with Marjie. She's working in her dad's office and likes it. Fanny came up this afternoon, and we fooled around, popped some pop-corn and etc. Rainy day.

Oh yes! I forgot to say, Fanny and I were looking through *Arts Oregana*,[69] and we found out that our Service Station Boy goes to U. of O. Is a soph[omore]. Belongs to the Chi Phis and his name is Murray Burns. Also, my Bob at Crater Lake is named Mr. Robert Foster and belongs to Art's fraternity. Some class, eh wot!!

Wednesday, August 18

Went to a show with Fanny and Judy. Not bad. Judy's cute. I like her. Got a new hat. Could be worse. Life is dull.

Lunchtime break for Rae Bailey at the Portland Lumber Company mill, circa 1920. Rae and many of Doris's friends got summer jobs.

---

[69] The University of Oregon yearbook.

Thursday, August 19
I went down town and met Marjie. Saw that darn little snob Jean that goes to the [St. Helen's] Hall. I dread school for that reason. I met Dick Detzi[e] formally today. Joe introduced me. He seems to like me, but I don't like his profile when I get close to it. Rather cute, tho. He said that Fred Y. was working at Long View.[70]

SS Exam[71] tomorrow. Oh!

Gene came over this evening. It was good to see him. He's just as silly as ever and simply wild about Marjie.

Friday, August 20
Marjie came in, and Gene came over as per-usual. Danced and fooled around. Fanny and Art came over for a while. Art is terribly sophisticated and tries to act so damned old. Just because he's a Freshman at college, he thinks he's a big egg. Why, Bob Foster didn't act half as old, and he's a Junior. Bob and Artis came over for a while, too. I rather like Gene. He wasn't *nearly* as sarcastic as he sometimes is.

Saturday, August 21
Fanny and I had the car for a while this afternoon. We went down to our filling station. Had a *very* good time. You know what I mean. Murray Burns was fired, but the other one was there and exceedingly attentive. Ah!!

Marjie came in again this evening, and we went to a show. Forgot to say that Gene came over in [the] afternoon and coolly informed me that he had read my other diary from start to finish. The damn fool. Can you beat it? And I raved about Micky bloody murder. I blush every time I look at him.

---

70 Longview, in southern Washington, was one of the first planned communities, built in 1921 to house workers for the lumber mills and yards there.
71 Sacred Studies.

~~Luckily I didn't have~~ And it *is* embarrassing. It's things like that which make me wonder if it's safe to keep a diary? I hope he doesn't broadcast everything he read. I'll be afraid to say anything now for fear someone will read it.

Sunday, August 22

Gee, but I had fun today. Mrs. Dana phoned early this morning and asked Marjie and me to come straight out there. That they were going on a picnic. We didn't expect to have much fun but went anyway. We went to some funny old ranch close to Salem.[72] It was apparently a regular family reunion because there were 25 people. All relatives of Marjie's. Anyway, there was one adorable boy that I had fun with. He dared us to ride a little 2-year-old colt that was unbroken. So we donned some old overalls and rode him. He bucked like Hell, and I had a heck of a time sticking on him. But I did and that's that.

Doris adored pets her entire life, including Fritz the Spitz (pictured, page 186) and this unnamed kitty.

---

[72] The capital of Oregon, about forty-seven miles south of Portland on the Willamette River.

Monday, August 23

Fanny and I took the Ford and went down town to our S.S. [service station]. I like Max *almost* as well as Murray. My new kitten came today, and it is adorable. I named her Valentia. Isn't that cute? Gee, but I am crazy about it.

Tuesday, August 24

Went down town with Fanny. Then met Marjie and we went to the Oaks[73] (Marjie and I). There was a [formal] picnic or something like that. When we were going down the Blue Streak, two adorable boys played a uke in back of us. After that, they took us on the—something or other. About that time Mrs. Merrick came over. "Oh, I see you've introduced yourselves," she said. *That* was lucky. After that, they took us to the dance. Both of them are cute as heck. We had a *marvelous* time, and they invited us to the Nat.

Wednesday, August 25

We went to Nat.[74] and oh boy. Fun fun fun. Beuferd and Gordon are their names. Ages 20 and 21. I feel exhilarated. Beuferd is cuter'n heck. Awfully nice to me, too, and flattering. Whoopee!

Thursday, August 26

Had the Ford and bummed around. Went down town. Fanny came up this evening. I crave excitement.

Friday, August 27

Same old thing. Damn!!

---

73 The Oaks amusement park, the oldest in Portland, the so-called Coney Island of the Northwest, is still running. It opened in 1905 to coincide with the Lewis and Clark Centennial.

74 The Natatorium, a swimming pool.

Saturday, August 28

Went down town and read to Mr. Dana. Then came home with him. I *love* Marjie so.

Sunday, August 29

[The] Reynolds came, and we went for a picnic. Ed is rather cute. I played croquet with him all afternoon. We also went swimming. I think Ed likes me. I like him. Goodness! I'm writing my diary briefly lately. Oh well. I never have anything to say anyway.

Rae's friends at the Clackamas River picnic in 1918.

Monday, August 30

Came home this morning. Mother told me to take [the] Ford and go to [the] store. As I was backing out of the Garage, I bumped into the ice wagon. Thrilling!! Then I skidded halfway down the hill. Took it again in the afternoon and got Fanny. We went to see S.S.M.[?] Had fun. Gene came over this evening. We fooled around. He says he doesn't like Marjie anymore because he abhors ice-bergs. That settled it for me. I'm never going to be cool to a boy. It doesn't work.

I crave romance! Thrills! Adventure! Will this boresome [*sic*] life never cease?

Tuesday, August 31
We went to the Rotary picnic today (Danas and I). In the evening there was a dance. They were having a Paul Jones,[75] and everyone was getting switched around. Who should I bump into but Murray Burns. Gee, I was surprised. I danced a couple with him. He's a *wonderful* dancer and cute as heck. I like him.

Wednesday, September 1
Just think! The first of September. In another week my freedom will be over, and I'll have to work work work. Darn!!! We went to a show tonight. Good. Also, a new maid came. She's fresh from the country and terribly dumb. Too innocent to live.

---

75 A Paul Jones is a mixer dance where switching partners is part of the fun.

**The maid, unidentified in this 1916 photo, could be Lily
or the new (unnamed) girl mentioned by Doris.**

Thursday, September 2

I went down town with Mother and got new shoes, new stockings, sweater, dress, purse, silk underwear. Not bad—that.

The maid acts kind of funny. I wonder if she is so innocent or she pretends. I dreamt about Micky last night.

Friday, September 3

Met Marjie down town, and we went to a show. Had a Sundae at Beck's. Mother and Daddy left for Wallowa Lake[76] this afternoon and won't be back until Tuesday. I'm left in complete charge of the house. Have to cook all meals. The new maid is so dumb she can't even fry bacon. It's going to be one hell of a weekend for me. I see that.

---

76 In eastern Oregon near the Idaho border.

I want my Micky so badly. I think about him all the time.

Alyce cut all the ligaments in her foot in an auto accident. Lucky!! I never have anything exciting like that happen to me.

Saturday, September 4

Oh, but today has been one hell of a day. I'll start at the beginning. Rae said that I could use the car to go to Alyce's. I decided on impulse to go get Marjie and bring her in. So I did. Then the two of us went to Alyce's to learn the deadly details of the accident. So far so good. Then we started home.

We had gotten to 28th and Broadway when we had a puncture. Tried to change tires, but I guess we're unnaturally dumb. Anyway, it ended by walking two blocks for a garage man. He fussed around and finally changed it. Took my last fifty cents, too. We then had ten minutes to meet Rae. We dashed down town, and traffic was so thick I could hardly drive.

I don't know how it all happened, but a cop jumped on my running board and began bawling me out for disregarding traffic signals and blah blah! He asked for my driver's license, and of course I didn't have it with me. He looked stern and said, "Drive to [the] Police Station."

I said, "Why?" and he said, "You're under arrest!" Imagine it!!

A kind of chill settled over me, but I gave him my best smile and started ahead. On the way we picked up Rae. When we got there, he took me before a grouchy looking judge. He stalked forward and began to fire questions at me. "How old are you? Where is your driver's permit? Where do you live? How long have you been driving?" and blah blah.

Everything was so formal and direct. They made so much ado over nothing. I had the wildest impulse to giggle but managed to restrain it. He gave me a notice to appear next Tuesday and bring my driver's license. Now, I've lost my license. And even if I did find it, I have age 17 on it, and I told them I was 16. They'll make a big fuss about that. But I wouldn't mind it so badly if I could only find it.

They'll probably fine me $25 if I haven't it, and Daddy will have a fit. Oh!! I don't blame some people for committing suicide. It would be so simple if I would just quietly die tonight. Damn!! What *am* I going to do? The crazy judge raved on about a state penalty and etc. What *will* I do?

Gene came over tonight.

Sunday, September 5
Marjie and I went for a hike in MacClay[77] Park today. Gene came over this ~~afternoon~~ evening. We had fun. Gene, as usual, acted silly, and it made me forget next Tuesday.

Monday, September 6
Marjie left this morning. Gene came over this afternoon and stayed and stayed. Also Billy Bader. Billy's gotten rather cute. Gene didn't act so worse himself.

The folks came home this evening. I haven't told them yet about tomorrow. I'm going to try and talk the judge out of it. Here's hoping for the impossible.

Tuesday, September 7
Well, I talked the judge out of it. I had to argue for a whole hour but won eventually. And when I left, he actually smiled and wished me luck. That was one narrow escape all right.

---

77 Macleay Park, at 29th Avenue and Upshur Street.

Wednesday, September 8

School started today. Bah, how I hate it. I've got a stiff course [load], too. Fannie's coming to the Hall, tho. That's one thing in favor of it.

Thursday, September 9

I have a rotten course. Uninteresting subjects and etc. Fanny is going to get over heavy. I wish I wasn't so dumb.

Friday, September 10

Dumb day, blah!!!

Saturday, September 11

I met Marjie down town, and we went to see "Stella Dallas," a wonderful show. We spent all our money for it, tho, and had to walk home. I saw a boy I met at Crater Lake and talked to him. I saw he was lonesome and alone, and I was too darn dumb to ask him up until he had gone. We went on a ways and met Gordon. Talked to him a while and came home. Dressed. Went to Broadway Theater. That's all!!

Sunday, September 12

Marjie and I went out to her house this morning. Went down to beach. Canoeing and etc. Didn't see Fridze—D——!! Saw Glen, tho, and a bunch of others. One awfully cute one. Marjie insisted on coming home about 3 o'clock, tho, so we had to sit around the house the remainder of the afternoon. I wish I could go to Lincoln! I *hate* St. Helen's Hall. I dread tomorrow, with Chapel and its bunch of superfluous girls. Darn!!

Tuesday, September 14

Gene came over this evening, and we sat on the porch and talked. Mother kept switching the light on, which was very silly. Since it was Gene whom I was with. He's terribly frank and oh so conceited. He's got it into his foolish head that all the girls are in love with him. Maybe he'll grow out of it. I don't see what Marjie sees in him, tho.

Enough for Gene!! It's Micky who I love with all my heart. He probably isn't half as crazy about me, but that doesn't keep me from loving him. He is so sweet.

Wednesday, September 15

I have an awful cold. Isn't it queer how drab some things can be and how perfectly exotic others are? Like, for example, the desert. When the sun has just disappeared behind a range of dun-colored hills, making of the sky a perfect mass of colors. The desert moon has just risen and travels majestically across the sky. The cattle have ceased to fight the flies, and wild bands of horses have settled themselves for the night. A quiet has descended upon the universe, and silence reigns supreme. This is Paradise. Where a man may go and find peace of soul in the great solitude of the desert. This is where true love is born, never to die. Ah! A dance-floor with the handsomest man in town to lavish attention upon one cannot be nearly as romantic as a homely, but clean outspoken cowboy and the desert.

That is romance, and I have to have a cold.

[untitled]⁷⁸

Beautiful eyes, wonderful hair

Awfully conceited, goes everywhere,

Careless of lessons, never has any,

Beautifully built, accomplishments many.

His kisses are perfect, from practice, they say,

But kisses are cheap when they're given away.

A cynical smile, evil and sweet,

That gives you a thrill to the soles of your feet.

Can be awfully naughty,

Can be awfully nice,

Makes you feel like a furnace, surrounded by ice.

---

78 This poem seems to be Doris's original.

I'm in love with love.

Chasm of oblivion ...

Since other diary:

1	18	Micky Stevens (He'll <u>always</u> be first)[79]
2	19	Murray Burns (a Chi Phi at U of O. Cute!)
3	18	Dick Detzi (Fred Yarnell's chum)
4	21	Bob Foster (an *adorable* college boy)
5	20	McClusky (man)
6	20	Beuferd (a life guard!!!)

---

[79] She doesn't explain the number rankings in her boy-lists, but this list seems to be in order of preference, with ages.

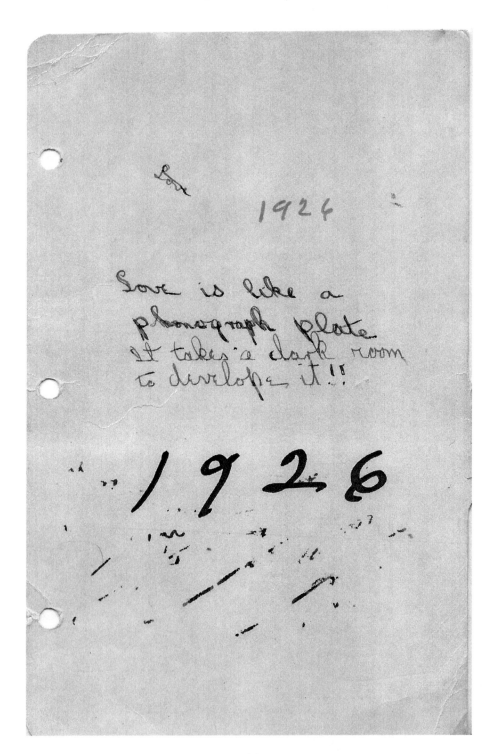

Love

1924

Love is like a
phonograph plate
It takes a dark room
to develop it!!

1926

I'll laugh at this world as I see it.[80]

Its women, its cities, its men.

I'll smile again as a cynic,

Who, embittered, sees only the evil in men.

For you have broken and shattered my heart,

And my soul is withered and white,

I hate you! I hate you! I hate you!

But oh! How I miss you tonight.

Dedicated to Micky

---

[80] This unattributed poem, which is not Doris's original, also appeared in the *Cornell Daily Sun*, December 20, 1928.

Wednesday, September 15

Well, I've changed diaries once and for all.[81] This one is going to last til I'm through school. It's terribly inconvenient to have to change every three or four months. It always leaves a gap and so forth. I hope by the time I finish this that it will be *full* of excitement and romance. Here's hoping for the best.

Thursday, September 16

Went to school as usual. There were a whole gang of Lincoln boys on the car this morning. Cute! This afternoon I took the car down and got Jack a Dixie.[82] On my way back I saw Hale and Dick Allen. Both waved and acted awfully glad to see me. I thought Hale might phone this evening, but he didn't. Worse luck!

Friday, September 17

School, blah!! This afternoon I had the Ford and went down below the hill. Who should I see but Bob Stryker. He got in with me, and we drove around. He said something about Evaline. "Oh, so you're still going with Evaline!" I said and then he said, "Yes, I think I'll marry Evaline!" Just like that. I was so surprised I just stared at him. Why, he is barely 19 and she's only 17. They're both silly, and I told him so.

He said something else, too, and it was that Jack Hibbard had joined the Navy. Now both Micky and Jack are on the ocean. Gee, but it's awful. Two boys that I like so well for [being so] far away. Wouldn't it be funny if I married a sailor?

But Jack was a fool. A sailor's life is hard, and he's just a little weakling. I like him, tho. It came as something of a shock, to know that I wouldn't see him anymore.

---

81 Doris's quip on the frontispiece to the fourth diary says, "Love is like a phonograph plate; it takes a dark room to develope [*sic*] it!" She means *photograph* plate.
82 Probably a brand of candy.

Billy and Leslie came up this evening. We went for a ride, and Billy kissed me. Gee, but it seemed funny. He was so damned amateurish about it that it seemed almost funny.

Saturday, September 18

Went down town and got my hair curled. I saw Dick Detzi[e] and a fat boy. Came out to Marjie's and we acted silly. Gee, but I love her.

Sunday, September 19

Went to Sunday School and Church. Had an *awful* time keeping awake. Went canoeing this afternoon and saw Butch. Had a very good time. ~~Gene~~ I came home this evening, and Gene came over. Here's the big surprise. *He kissed me*!!! Not only once, but twice. He hasn't kissed me for *ages*. Gee, but I was surprised. And he had improved marvelously. Why, his kisses were almost thrilling. In fact, they *were* thrilling. Now I'm beginning to realize why Marjie is so crazy about him. Tho I could never like him like she does. He's too cynical and conceited. Cute looking, tho, and he does kiss nicely. But it's Micky I love. He is so wonderful. No wonder I don't like any of the boys. I compare them all with him, and of course they fall short. No one could even hold a candle to him. But when I compare Gene and Fritzie, why, I begin to see that Gene isn't so bad, blah—

What am I arguing about anyway? What difference does it make whether Gene's as nice as Micky or Fritzie as nice as Gene? It's silly, blah—I'm going to quit.

Monday, September 20

I'm in love. But it's one-sided and he doesn't even know my name, so what difference does it make? I see him on the street car every morning. His name is Frank Norris. He's a Secret Sorrow if there ever was one.

Tuesday, September 21
Same as usual. Took the Ford this afternoon and saw Bob Stryker again. Also three other Hill boys. I keep thinking of Frank Norris. I wish I could get acquainted with him.

Wednesday, September 22
After school I took the Ford and went down to the Service Station. They acted awfully cute and were really flattering. Man wanted a date!!!

Thursday, September 23
Had Ford again this afternoon. Gene came over this evening all dressed up in new hat, suit, shoes. He kissed me once while I was phoning. Then when I was studying at my desk, he came in, said, "Goodby, Doris," and kissed me twice. I don't understand it. I know he doesn't like me. He's in love with Marjie, and I know I don't like him. I'm in love with Micky. Still, he does kiss nicely, so I haven't objected as yet. I'll ease my conscience by telling Marjie. I'd be mad if Fritzie kissed her, but it's different with Gene. I hope.

Friday, September 24
I came out to Marjie's this afternoon. Her folks have gone to Eugene,[83] and we have the house to ourselves. We were just getting ready for bed when Gene and Joe drove up. They stayed until about 12.

Saturday, September 25
Marjie came in with me this morning. This afternoon we served at a tea for a bunch of old women. Gee, but it was dumb. This evening a bunch of Hill boys came up. Also Evaline, Margie S., and Vie. There were 10 of [us] altogether.

---

83 Eugene is 111 miles south of Portland at the southern end of the Willamette River Valley.

We really had an awfully good time. Gene stood around and acted kind of dumb, but Hale was cute. Bob is really engaged. He told me so again tonight, and he's crazy about her. I don't think she likes him very well, tho. Then there was a new boy named Jerry something. Oh, but he was cute. 6 ft. 3 [inches] and *handsome*—black curly hair, big blue eyes, and everything. Oh, but *he's big*. Looks like Jack Dempsey.[84] A real he-man if there ever was one. And a foot-ball hero. He's full-back on the team and everything. He's the type I could marry. Tall, muscular, thrilling, wonderful dancer and etc. The kind that should be out in the mountains in a soft flannel shirt open at the throat and on a horse. Gee, but I'm *crazy about him*. He's so ideal.

About 12 o'clock [midnight] we all went for a ride and parked. I didn't like that very well, it spoiled the effect. Especially since he didn't kiss *me*. But he was thrilling just the same. When he looks at me, my knees feel weak and my heart pounds. He's a *perfect boy*, as I've said before.

Sunday, September 26

We took Mother to church today. Then went up to see Alyce. She looks so thin. Has lost at least 10 pounds and is pale. This afternoon we went for a walk. She left about 6:30, and just after she had gone, Gene came over. We went into the music room and talked. He likes her pretty well, I guess. He wasn't so bad to me. Was really flattering at intervals. He's a good kid but conceited. He stayed until 9.

Monday, September 27

They almost let me take the car to school today but not quite. I played tennis today and knocked the ball over the fence. As I was climbing over it, I caught my skirt and ripped it. Worse luck!

---

84 Professional boxer who held the World Heavyweight Championship from 1919 to 1926.

Saw Gene today at Bernie's and brought him up the hill. (I had used the car to go to the library.) That's all that happened. Dull life.

I feel romantic tonight. But of course, there isn't a romance. Thrills and adventures have a habit of avoiding me. The only way I can have any excitement is to use my imagination. I weave all kinds of thrilling experiences, but that's all the good it does me. Damn!

I say it again. Damn!! And I mean it. Here I am just dying for adventures and nothing happens. Nothing! Nothing!! Nothing!!! I'm sick of it.

Now here comes Gene bounding up the stairs. I'm glad my door is shut. I can't stand his sarcasm. Especially when I want my Micky. Gene seems so shallow and cynical. Micky is so clean and good and romantic. If he were here, maybe I wouldn't be longing for romance. But he isn't here, and I get tired of dreaming about him when he is so fast becoming a vague figure. He'll be just a myth before long, and I don't want a myth and a vague dream. I want something in the present. Now!! I wish I'd meet some cute boy, and he'd fall in love with me. I'm kind of funny, I guess. I'll bet no boy will even want to marry me. I'll most likely be an old maid. Damn!!!! What's the use?

Tuesday, September 28
We had a class meeting today and elected President, Vice President, and Secretary. Med. Roberts got Pres. Gee, I was glad. She deserves it if anyone does.

Fanny acted so funny today. About second period I saw her phoning. She seemed to be arguing about something. I didn't think much about it but went on down to "Study Hall." About the middle of the period when everything was quiet, the door opened and in walked Fanny. She slammed the door and clattered down the aisle. It seemed almost sacrilegious to disturb the silence, but it didn't seem to bother her. She stamped to her seat. Slammed her books on her desk. Knocked her chair over. Sat it up with a bang and plopped down in it. Put her chin between her hands and began to cry. Pretty soon she quieted down and went up to English with me. About the middle of the English period, she burst out bawling and left the room. I wonder what it's all about. She isn't usually so—well, emotional.

Wednesday, September 29
Stayed home from school today. Will probably have a lot to make up when I go back. Saw Hale today. He looked cute. Also saw Jerry from afar. I wonder if Margie S. is going to invite me to her party. She ought to, but I haven't seen any signs of it as yet.

Thursday, September 30
Fanny wasn't at school today. Hasn't been since that day she cried and acted so funny. After school today, Judy and I went down to the Hazelwood[85] for a soda. There's a cute boy down there named John. We had an awfully good time, giggled and so forth. I like Judy. She's full of pep and lots of fun. I saw Bob S. today coming up on the car. I *don't* see what Evaline wants to marry him for. He's so *dumb* looking.

Friday, October 1
Rae let me take the Ford to school today. Took it at lunch time. After school, Judy and I drove down to the Hazelwood and got a Sundae. Then I drove Judy up here, and we monkeyed around. Went to see Fanny. She says she's been sick. Went to a show this evening. Pretty good. Margie invited me to her party, but I don't think I'll go. She says Tom Kennedy would be my partner, and I don't like him.

---

85 A neighborhood/district in Portland, possibly a specific café there.

The Bailey house was a magnet for school friends. Here, Rae and fellow members of the Lincoln High School Zip Jazz Quartet cut up with friend Penelope G.

Saturday, October 2

Mother and I went down town about 10 o'clock today. We shopped until 3. I got a new hat. Then I took Mother home. Took the car and went over to Alyce's. Talked to her a while and went over to Margie's. I had intended telling her that I couldn't come tonight, but she said that Tom wasn't coming, so I decided I would go.

On the way back I stopped at a different gas station, and Walt Heitkeimper was there. He acted so nice and asked me to come in again. I'm going to, too. I like him, and I'm getting sick of Mac. This evening Joe, Gene, and I went over to Margie's in the Ford. She had an awfully good bunch. Bob Clancy and Jerry included. Also a new boy named Carl Anderson. Everything started off with a bang until Jerry and Grimes began to wish for something to drink. Bob and Joe took the Ford and went to get some.

In the meantime, Carl said he wanted to get acquainted with me, so we went out on the porch and got acquainted. He isn't so bad. About 11 o'clock, tho, her folks came home. Just after they had gotten home, Joe drove up. The boys went outside to tip them off, which was lucky because they had a quart.

Mr. Schmorl said that if we wanted to, we could all pile in his car and go get some Barbecue Sandwidges [sic]. So Joe, Gene, Evaline, and Bob took the Ford. The rest of us got in the big car. Jerry, however, had taken a little too much and began to sing. We tried to drown him out, but I think Mr. Schmorl caught on. He didn't say anything, tho. We all piled into the Sandwidge [sic] Shop and got something to eat. Jerry was screamingly funny and kept us all laughing. After that we all came home. It was about 1:30 [a.m.], tho, before we got here because we had a blow out. I like Bob Clancy. He's different. He didn't get drunk, either. But all things considered, we had an awfully good time.

Sunday, October 3
I washed my hair this afternoon, and Gene came over before I had curled it. He said he liked it straight and that I ought to leave it that way. Maybe I will. It saves $1 a week, and I don't mind that. Think of all I could buy with that dollar. I can't keep my mind off of Walt today. Crazy, isn't it? When I barely know him.

Monday, October 4
Dull day. Nothing happened. I have an awful headache.

Tuesday, October 5
School as usual. Today in English Fanny and I got the giggles. We got the whole class to laughing and had an awful time. I got up to recite, and Fanny sat in the back and grinned. It was awful!!!!!

Wednesday, October 6

Chapel was quite dull as usual this morning. In the first place, two of the dumbest girls in school sat in front of us. Harriet and I decided to make them mad, so we pulled their veils behind the seat and tied the corners together. The whole row was giggling about it. Then they got up to sing, and of course their veils stayed by the seat. They reached down and grabbed them and tried to put them on before Sister saw. We were all in convulsions, and Fanny let out a screech. We had just quieted down, and the Bishop was trying to pray. For some reason or other he forgot his lines and just quit talking. There was dead silence, and then we began to giggle again. I guess because it was so serious. Sister frowned at us, and then the choir droned, "A—men."

By that time the Bishop had waken up [*sic*] and began where he left off. Which was silly because the "Amen" had already been said. Of course, that started us off afresh, and we all laughed until we cried. It seemed as tho we just couldn't stop and then—lo and behold, Dorothy Rogers fainted. Maxine took her out, and Chapel was adjourned for the day. Too much excitement for Sister, I guess. Everything considered, it wasn't so bad. Ardean said she was going to tell Superior about the veils, but she apparently didn't.

I want to go to the Oregon-Washington game[86] so badly. No chance, tho.

Thursday, October 7

We had a Masquerade at school this evening. Just before I left, I went in to show the maid my costume, and there sat the best looking man! She's kind of funny looking. I don't see how she got him. Mustache and everything. We had a good time at the party. Of course there were only girls, but we had a five piece orchestra, and all the musicians were good looking. There

---

86 The game was played on Saturday, October 9, 1926. Portland's Multnomah Civic Stadium was dedicated that day. Doris would have been disappointed; Washington beat Oregon, 23–9.

was a crowd of girls around the orchestra *all* the time. Sister gave us some dirty looks but didn't say anything.

Friday, October 8

I was on the deficiency list for SS [Sacred Studies] today. Fanny was, too. After we had stayed our hour, we went to the Hazelwood and got a Sundae. The boys in there *are* cute. Then I came home. When I came home, Mother said that I was to go out to Marjie's. So I changed my stockings and went. So here I am. Gee, but I love her.

Saturday, October 9

Marjie and I came in this morning. We ate lunch at Beck's and went to a show. Then we walked up by the Stadium and stood around listening to the cheers. It made us so jealous. I never wanted to see a foot ball game so badly before. I guess we must have looked pretty forlorn, because a boy said, "Do you girls want to go to the game? Here's a ticket." Of course we didn't take it, but oh, temptation!! Gene came over this evening. Marjie is disgustingly crazy about him.

Sunday, October 10

We got up really early this morning, and the four of us went for a hike. We really had an awfully good time. We went the same way that we went with Micky that time. Memories!

Oh! Mother let Marjie and me take the car to church. I saw Walt Heitkeimper, and he waved to me. I like him awfully well. There's something thrilling about his blue eyes. I'd like to get to know him better. We went over to see Alyce and then to church. It was Communion Sunday and supposed to be very serious. Of course we got the giggles and laughed and laughed. It was awful! It's misery to laugh hard anyway. But to laugh like that in church when you have to do it silently. Oh!! This afternoon we went for a walk and ended up at the show. Tho we shouldn't have. Felt guilty. Rainy day.

Monday, October 11
Oh! How I hate *Mondays*!!!

Tuesday, October 12
I got some new galoshes today. Also took the Ford down below the hill. That's all!!

Wednesday, October 13
Had a SS [Sacred Studies] test today, and I know I flunked in it. But I got A in a book report, and my English teacher said that I had "Literary Ability"—*ah-ah*! Played basket ball and got a bloody nose. The ball hit me square on the lip of it. Took Ford to do some errands for Mother. I stopped in front of Bernie's, and the damn thing wouldn't start again. Johnny Leverton (who I knew at Lincoln but hadn't seen since last fall) cranked[87] it for me. He is without question the best looking boy I've ever known. Big blue eyes and etcetera. I'm falling. We talked a long time, but he isn't interested enough. Didn't even ask for my phone number. Damn! Just my luck. After that I killed my engine in front of a drug store, and a nice Englishman with a mustache said, "Can I be of assistance?" So he cranked it for me. Wasn't that nice? The next time I killed it was at a STOP street[88], and a good looking brunette cranked it for me. I resolved never again to drive that car until the battery was fixed. Stopped in at W. Heitkeimper's service station. Like him!!

---

87 Early automobiles had to be cranked to start the engine, before electric starters and keys became commonplace.
88 Stop sign at an intersection.

Thursday, October 14

This morning I got on the street car, and Fanny was there, naturally. We were talking away, and Elizabeth Berger got on the car. She goes to [St. Helen's Hall] and is rather nice in a back number way. I moved over for her to sit with us, and to my surprise Fanny slid so that she couldn't sit down. Made a face at me, telling me she didn't want Elizabeth to sit with us. I didn't want to snub her cold, so I invited her to sit down. She did. Then Fanny stuck up her nose and said, "*I'm* going to sit in back." Just then Louise got on, and she said, "Come on, Louise, *we'll* sit back here today." It was all so obvious, it was embarrassing. It is almost *unbelievable* that such people can be such snobs and get away with it. It is so *little*, so mercenary. So disgusting. I've never been quite so mad at Fanny before. Because they have a little more money than most people, she thinks she is better than Elizabeth. Why, no one is better than anyone else, and if someone is lucky enough to have money, why oh why do they become snobbish? Life is a farce!! By fourth period Fanny had the nerve to smile gaily at me as if nothing had happened.

Bu something *did* happen. Fanny has hurt Elizabeth's feelings and made her miserable. I'm glad I sat with her anyway. It has proven to me just what Fanny is like with the veneer rubbed off. Enough for Fanny and Elizabeth!!

This afternoon Johnny Leverton was down at the car-line. We talked to him for a long time. Once he made a motion as if to step on my foot. As I cringed, he said, "Why, what's the matter? I wouldn't hurt you for the world." His voice was so soft and low. Almost a caress. And once, oh, once we were talking about people dancing on other people's feet, and he said, "Let's try it!" and held out his arms. My poor little heart went bump bump bump! I took his hands and put my feet on his. We walked like that a while, and his nearness was—well, intociccating [*sic*]. He *is* so cute!! And his eyes! Oh.

Friday, October 15

I was on the deficiency list, and so I didn't get to 23rd in time to see Johnny. Darn. The McCords came for dinner, and after dinner the Mathis[es] came. About 8 o'clock Marjie, Evaline, Ruth, and a bunch of boys phoned and wanted to come up. And I couldn't have them because the folks were playing cards. And Joe Burton was going to be my partner. Damn. And I had to play *bridge* and get sleepy. Oh! Life is cruel, but they're all coming tomorrow night, so it could be worse.

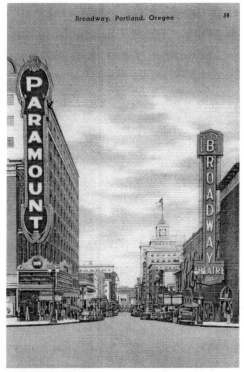

**Portland's Broadway was the place to go to see
a live vaudeville show or a movie.**

Saturday, October 16

I drove Mother down town this morning. This afternoon I went over to Marjie's, and we went to Evaline's. The three of us were going to see the

"Black Arab,"[89] but it was too crowded. So we decided to come out to the Nob Hill.[90] We did, and after we had been seated a while, Bob Stryker and two other boys appeared. Bob introduced them as Larry Lenate and Leo Thorten. Both of them perfectly adorable.

After the show, the six of us piled in the Ford and came up to my house. We danced and monkeyed around. Leo has black hair and brown eyes. Awfully full of pep. Larry—oh, Larry—I can't keep it any longer. I am crazy about him. He has soft brown hair that is in delightful disorder. His eyes are a clear steady blue. The color of Crater Lake. He has a wonderful complexion, and the whole effect is one of jaunty, devil-may-care. So boyish and exuberant. And he has wonderful manners. I love boys that have nice manners. They're such a relief from the way Gene acts. I took them down to Hill about 5:30 and from there went to have the battery recharged. Marjie came home and had dinner with me.

After dinner, Ruth C., Dick Stevens, Eveline, Bob, Gene, *and* Larry came up. We did have fun. Marjie wasn't very popular. Gene sat around. But Steve played the uke, and Larry sang in his deep but boyish voice. After that we danced, and I played blackjack with Larry. Oh, I'm so crazy about him. He is so different from the common horde. He has personality and loads and loads of character. I like him! Oh, I like him so. His eyes, his eyes, oh his eyes. He's my ideal.

Sunday, October 17
I took Evaline back this morning and went to church. Got terribly sleepy as usual. On the way home I passed Leo, and he waved and smiled. He's fairly brimming over with pep. I never saw anything like it. I was going to Evaline's this afternoon, but Mother made me study. I wasn't surprised. This evening Gene came over, and we went for a walk.

---

89 She must mean *The Arab*, a 1924 film.
90 Cinema at Kearney Street and 23rd Avenue.

Monday, October 18

Played tennis fourth period with Fanny. This afternoon we saw Johnny Leverton. He's cute as hell, but he'll have to go some to beat Larry. I also saw Steve Prothero, who is ~~also cute~~ adorable. But I'm simply crazy about Larry. I can't get him out of my mind.

Tuesday, October 19

Almost late to Chapel today but got there just in time. Darn. This afternoon Sister Superior called an Assembly. She began with, "The school has been disgraced, and blah blah." She raved on and on and finally by the time she had [us] all wondering what in H—— she had on her mind, she said, "There is, in this room, a girl who is a thief. A low-down, common, ordinary thief." The room was deadly quiet. Then she went on to say that this girl had stolen dollar bills, fountain pens, and even jewelry. She *knew* who she was and etc. I looked around to see if anyone was blushing, but I couldn't see. Sister talked for half an hour, and by the time she quit, she had us all feeling as if she suspected us.

I have my suspicions, tho, as to who the girl is. *Jean Morrison*. She'd be capable of it, and she acted awfully funny. She hardly ever talks to Fanny and me, but after Assembly she came up to us and said, "Do you know who it is? I wonder who it is? How did Sister know, I wonder?" and etc. Fanny and I are going to do some detective work and discover the culprit. You watch us.

Wednesday, October 20

Had *two* tests today, and I know I flunked in both. Got an invitation to the Hill dance. Whoopee!! Also got two ADORABLE new dresses. I would be perfectly happy now if only Larry would phone. Oh well. I'll see him at the dance. Played tennis!! Gene came over this evening.

Thursday, October 21

Another test today and two tomorrow. Oh! I saw Margaret Denham down town today. She looked awfully tough and common. Fanny snubbed her, but I forced myself to talk to her. Oh, how did I ever stand her? Saw Virgil Goodwin while we were waiting for the car, and the girls dared me to say "hello" to him. I did, and to my surprise, he said, "Hello, Doris!" Will wonders never cease? Alyce phoned me this evening. She's cute. Said that she talked to Mais Brown today. Lucky dog.

Friday, October 22

I felt like hell today. Called Evaline up this morning. She said that Bob said that Larry said that "he was off of women." Encouraging, isn't it? Saw Leo this afternoon. He's cute. Went for a walk with Fanny this evening. I'm blue. Want something to do. Darn! If something doesn't happen!!

After I had written this, Bob and Chauncy came up. Bob's rather cute.

Saturday, October 23

This morning I took Joe over to Chauncy's. Chauncy's brother, him, Joe, and myself went down to the boat. Gilbert is adorable. Little mustache and everything. Acted interested, too, umm! I like him. Then I took Joe home. On the way I saw Larry, but he doesn't like me. Damn! He's cute, too. Then I hide [hied[91]] myself to the dentist and suffered for half an hour. As I came out of the office, a nice looking boy was sitting in the waiting room. He smiled and said, "Why, hello, Doris!"

I didn't know who it was, so I just said, "Hello." He acted kind of taken [a]back, but he said, "How's school?" I *couldn't* imagine who he was, so I just said, "Oh, pretty good" and turned to put my hat on. Just then, the Doctor came out and said, "Come in, Bud."

---

91 Went quickly.

Then I realized, but it was too late. He was just going into the office. I met him at C.L.P.,[92] and we got to know each other awfully well that night. He probably thinks I was snubbing him. Oh darn! I never *can* remember faces until too late. After all this I came out to Marjie's. She met me in her car. We saw Fritzie, and he waved. He is so cute. Sat around and read this evening.

Sunday, October 24
We went to S.S. [Sunday School] this morning. Dumb! Joan came down on her horse this afternoon. Lucky. Rae brought me home, and oh, of all that happened at home while I was gone. Of course it's just my luck. I'll go for weeks and not have any excitement. Then the minute I exit from the scenery, variety appears.

Rae said that some boy called me up, but he couldn't remember his name. Brothers are so helpful. Then Joe said that Johnny Leverton had been up Saturday afternoon and asked for me. I wasn't here, so they went for a walk, and Gene said (and if he says it, it *must* be true) that Johnny said that I had a cute little baby face (*imagine* it!), and he liked me better than Fanny, AND if he had his way about it, he'd be up here oftener. Isn't that *wonderful*? Also, Evaline phoned and was having a party and wanted me to come. She probably would have had Larry and everything. Darn, I *do* have the worst luck.

Mother fell down the steps this evening and scared us all half to death.

Monday, October 25
Gee! There's a lot of excitement today at school. Frances James is 22 years old (we thought she was only 16). She is a *bigamist*. And one of her husbands is accused of white slavery. *Isn't* that *awful*? I always thought she was kind of sneaky and funny. Sister found some weird letters and investigated.

---

92 Unclear, but probably a church activity.

Last night when Frances got expelled, she got Mary Elizabeth Huron in a corner and tried to choke her. Poor Elizabeth was scared to death. She's half-cracked and plain ordinary everyday immoral. Sister is afraid it will get back to the school and give [St. Helen's Hall] a bad name. That *would* be awful.

Tuesday, October 26
Went to a foot ball game today. Grant won, 7–0. Pretty good, isn't it? Saw Alyce and Marjie. Alyce acted awfully high-hat. Marjie was just her own sweet self.

Willie Doris (Upshaw) Bailey in her Scripps-Booth, which Rae jokingly called her "Slips Loose," 1919. When Mother wanted a new car, she got one. Joe is in the car, too.

Wednesday, October 27
Felt like H—— today. Had Ford in afternoon. There was a man here trying to sell Mother a Chev. Sedan. Hope she buys a Chev. Coup[e] instead.

Marjie phoned me this evening. I don't understand her. She is changing so much. She has even been *deceiving* me lately. Gene was going out there, and she didn't tell me. She must not trust me anymore. Our friendship is fading. I don't think I could live without her love, but I certainly don't intend to push myself. I dreamed last night that she died. Oh, it was *awful*. Just as if a part of my life had gone, and yet—there is restraint between us. Not the same feeling of camaraderie that there was before. Although I love her *more* than ever. I wish she wasn't changing. I was so happy the way it was.

Thursday, October 28

School school school bah! I'm getting sick of it. I gave an oral report in English today, and the teacher said I had more poise than anyone she knew, and she wanted me to give an oral [report] before the whole assembly. *Imagine* it. Of course I'll be absent tomorrow. Defoe called me up this evening. So did Evaline. She wants me to go with a bunch tomorrow night and go out to the Oasis.[93] I might. There *is* a chance that it would be raided!! And that *would* be fun. Oh boy.

Friday, October 29

I stayed home from school to get my new dress made. Also to get some new shoes and a marcel. The shoes are adorable. Black satin strip pumps with heels this long [hand-drawn line 2 ¾ inches long]. That's not exaggerated either. I didn't go to the Oasis. Several reasons. Billy John and Leslie came up, and we went for a ride. Hot stuff!! Leslie's too bab[y]ish and Billy too sophisticated. Oh well!!

Oh say, this afternoon I was chugging up the hill with my little Ford, and a big black car dashed by me and honked. I looked, and it was Elaine Hickman. She *never* speaks to me at school, but just because I was in that

---

93 Crystal Springs Oasis was a "tea room" rumored to serve alcohol on the sly, on Sandy Boulevard.

little rattle trap and she in her big, black limousine, she had to show off. Damn. I was so mad at her I wanted to chew nails. Oh well! A Ford isn't so bad as all that. But I *do* wish Daddy would let me drive the big car.

Family friend Ruthmary Burroughs sits demurely in her dress and picture hat. Doris loved having new clothes.

Saturday, October 30

This afternoon Louise and I went to the game. Gee, but it was exciting. One man got his back broken; an ambulance came and everything. O.A.C. won, 3–0. This evening was the Hill dance. We all lined up upstairs and marched down to meet the boys as usual. I was hoping I'd meet Larry, but I didn't. Met some hick with a long nose. Just my luck. Anyway, after we'd been marching a while, the boy in front of me turned around. It was Larry. My poor little heart went *pitty pat skid skid.*

He said, "Why, hello, Doris. I haven't seen you in a long time." That was all. Then we danced, and I didn't see him until about the fifth dance. He came over and asked me. Oh! He dances wonderfully. And he *is* so cute. After that dance he danced with Harriet and danced and danced and danced. Oh! I had a good time, tho. Hale was exceptionally nice, and Leo made a date with me for Tuesday. Another boy, Bill Ragsdale, danced five or six with me, ate with me, and—well, appeared more than reasonably interested in me. Even jealous when I wouldn't sit out with him. He's coming up tomorrow. He's cute but doesn't compare with Larry. Damn! It makes me mad. Why couldn't Larry be as nice to me as Bill? Why couldn't *he* fall for me instead of Bill? Oh, the irony of fate. Harriet doesn't deserve him, and I *do* like him so.

Oh, say! A funny thing happened this evening. It was just as we were going out. I was standing in the hall talking to Billy, Hale, and Leo. Billy had one of my hands, and Lee the other. I was saying goodby to both of them, and Hale was trying to tell me something. Just then I turned around, and Mother and Daddy were standing there. I felt so foolish. Mother was glaring at me, and Dad was laughing. She thinks it's terrible for me to even smile at a boy. And when she saw me holding hands with two and flirting with another. Well—what didn't she say!!!

Sunday, October 31

Billy Ragsdale came up, and Rae took us over to Evaline's. Ruth, Dick, Bob, Margaret, and Basil Brown were there. Basil is adorable. We went for a ride out towards Beaverton.[94] Oh boy! Is Billy hot!!! There was a little too much necking, tho, and Basil isn't that kind. So we talked when we could. I like him. Billy gave me a compact. Nice of him, wasn't it? He made a date with me for next Sunday, but I don't think I'll keep it. I'd rather do something else. He's too young. Only seventeen.

---

94 Beaverton was seven miles west of Portland in the Tualatin River Valley.

Love

The Night has a thousand eyes,
And the Day but one;
Yet the light of the bright world dies
With the dying sun.

The mind has a thousand eyes,
And the heart but one;
Yet the light of a whole life dies
When love is done.[95]

Monday, November 1

Johnny Leverton got on the W.H.[96] street car this morning. He's cute as hell but conceited!!! Oh ye gods! School was dumb as usual. Harriet flaunted Larry's ring before the whole school. It's awful to think that that common little devil should have a ring with a magic "L" on it. How little did she realize with what pain I said, "Gee, that's a cute ring." Oh well. Jealousy is the root of all evil, so I'm not going to become jealous.

I had the Ford this afternoon and saw Leo. If I can get it tomorrow, he made me promise to take him for a ride. I like him. He's so darn full of pep. Also saw Billy. I felt kind of sick when I saw him. *Ohh*, how I hate him. I'm going to throw his compact away.

---

[95] By Francis William Bourdillon, but unattributed in the diary.
[96] The Willamette Heights car went from City Park to 23rd Avenue.

**Streetcars were the transportation mode of choice for
Doris and friends, unless she could get the car.**

Tuesday, November 2

I saw Johnny Leverton on the car again. He stopped and talked to us for
a while. In the afternoon I had the Ford and took Leo for his promised
ride. He made a date with me for Saturday. I don't like him as well as I
did. He's so coarse and unrefined. My mind and soul craves refinement
such as Larry and Micky. Gee, but I like Larry. Why couldn't it be him
that wanted the date? Leo kissed me. Not so worse.

Gene came over this evening. His folks weren't home, and he hadn't had
any dinner, so I heated some food for him. He got to acting silly and said,
"Look! I bet you can't do this!" and turned his plate over without spilling
anything. The second time, tho, it did spill all over the floor, and I had to
clean it up. Big fool.

Wednesday, November 3
Daddy took Marjie and me to [the] Broadway. It was an awfully good show.

Thursday, November 4
Played tennis, went to a foot ball game, and some college eggs sat in back of us. We got into a conversation with them, and it turned out that they went to U. of O. and knew Bob Foster *real* well. Hot dog!! We had fun, of course.

Friday, November 5
Took Ford this afternoon and killed the engine on Washington St. A nice man with a mustache cranked it for me. Daddy says I can have an orchestra for my party if I can get it for $5. He thinks I can't. But I will, you just see.

The bunch are coming over tomorrow night. It's the first time I've had a bunch and not had Hale. I thought I could get away with it, but this evening he phoned and said, "What's this I hear about you giving a party?" I told him, and he said, "Can I come too?" The cute thing. He's clever, and I rather like him. Larry's coming! Whoopee!!!! I had a date with Leo Thortery, but I broke it. Sure, why not? Love 'em and leave 'em! That's my motto.

Saturday, November 6
This afternoon I met Evaline and went to a show. She came home with me, and according to schedule, Bob and Leon were to come up. They did come—*but* brought Maloney and Jimmy Right. I hate Jimmy. The dirty little nut. But Maloney is adorable, and Leo isn't bad at all. We had a very good time, but Maloney accidentally broke the lamp and Bob, Mother's bowl. I don't know how I'll ever explain it. Damn!!

Sunday, November 7

This morning E. and I went to church and burnt out a bearing. Oh boy, but Rae was mad! I couldn't help it, tho. E. went home, and I fooled around with Gene. About 4 o'clock some boys phoned and asked if they could come up. I forgot to ask who they were, but I naturally thought it was Maloney and Bob. It wasn't, tho. It was Moody and Basil Brown. I needn't say that we enjoyed ourselves *immensely*. Moody had his car, and we went over and got E, Bob, and Margaret. Moody is so cute, and I got well acquainted with him. He doesn't talk so much, but what he does say is clever. And can he neck! Oh boy, talk about hot!! Wow!!!!!

Basil is cute as H—— but not so serious as he could be. Mother suspects something, but I couldn't help it if they came up. And we didn't do anything we shouldn't. Just had a good time. And Moody isn't a woman-hater anymore. Oh boy!!!

Monday, November 8

Played tennis. Dorothy Rogers got sick in Chapel again. Lucky dog! I wonder how she does it so often and gets away with it. I don't blame her for feeling sick, tho, when she looks at Father Clark. He'd make anyone feel faint. Got our report card[s] today. I got B in English, B in Eng. History, B in Art History, A in Tennis, and B in Elocution, but C in Sacred Studies. Oh well.

Tuesday, November 9

Saw Coe and Basil today. I think Basil is adorable.

Wednesday, November 10

This evening Hale phoned and said he had a pass until 10:30 and asked if he could come up. I said he could, so he did. We danced and made candy. He's awfully cute and acted really clever. He said that Moody was back at school. Isn't that nice? I'm not as glad as I should be, tho. Isn't it funny, you like a boy until he necks you. Then all the thrill is gone. Maybe that's why I like Larry and Micky so well.

Oh, say! I saw Johnny Leverton down town today. Talked to him a long time. He has the prettiest eyes of any boy I've ever seen. They're such a blue blue blue. And thrilling, too.

I'm going to give my party a week from Friday. Hope it comes out all right. I dread it. A dance is such a responsibility. I sent the invitations this evening.

Thursday, November 11

Gee! But I'm dumb!!! I hired the orchestra for the 20th instead of the 19th. After I had sent the invitations, I discovered my mistake and called up the orchestra. But they were engaged for the 19th!! And now I am in a nice fix! Everyone is invited, and I'm minus an orchestra. What'll I do? I had to hire them from my allowance, and they are the only ones that will fit it. Damn!!

Mother called up H.M.A. this afternoon to ask Mr. Hill if the [Hill] boys she invited were all right. He agreed to everyone but Bob S. He said Bob couldn't come if Evaline did because he had heard rumors that Evaline wasn't a *nice* girl. And that E. was a bad influence on Bob, and he was trying to break up the infatuation between them, and he didn't think Evaline was the kind of a girl Mother's daughter should associate with. Imagine it!!

Of course if rumors are going around about Evaline, I'll *have* to drop her because my reputation would be at stake if I didn't, and I don't want to ruin my reputation. Because it's the easiest thing in the world for a girl to get talked about. So be-ginning tonight, I'm off of Hill boys and necking. Of course, I've already invited some to my party, but after the party I'll drop the whole damn bunch of them. So there. Gee! I love Marjie D. When I compare her with Evaline and that gang, why, there's no comparison. She's so fine and such a true friend, and there's nothing like a true friend, and I love her so. She'd never get talked about. We went to the Music Box tonight. It was awfully clever.

Friday, November 12

We, that is, Fanny and I took the Ford this afternoon and went for a ride. Marjie came up this evening and said that last Wednesday she and Bob and Walt Heitkeimper went to the O.A.C. dance and they were coming up to get me, and they phoned me and I wasn't home, and darn it!! It would have been fun because Walt is cute as hell! She also said that my party invitations had been posted on the bulletin board at Hill. Darn. I didn't invite Billy Ragsdale, and I should have because he gave me a compact, and I didn't want him to know I was giving a party, but I don't care because he's nothing in my life, and I didn't compel him to give me a compact. And so if he doesn't like it, it's none of my business.

**Doris, right, called on her aunt Mae, left, to help
with the dance party orchestra problem.**

Saturday, November 13

We slept until 11 and then ate lunch. After that I took Mother down town, and Marjie and I had the Ford. We went over to Elizabeth P. and tried to get an orchestra. We couldn't, and I was discouraged about that, but we went out to Sellwood[97] to pay my bill at the Service Station and the boy was cute, so I wasn't quite so discouraged. Everyone seemed to be in a flirty mood today, so we had a good time. This evening Rae called [Aunt] Mae[98] up, and Mae said that maybe she could get an orchestra that would be within my allowance, so maybe everything will turn out all right after all.

Sunday, November 14

This has been one of the dumbest, dullest, most monotonous days of my life. I'm so bored I'm ready to commit a murder. It would make some excitement anyway. This time last Sunday I was in a car, seated beside Moody, talking, laughing, feeling gay because my secret sorrow had come to life. I thrilled every time his blue eyes flashed a smile at me. Every time he said some soft, caressing inconsequential compliment, I felt exhilarated. And after that magnificent ride, we came home, were standing in the kitchen, and he kissed me. Gently, tenderly, thrillingly, and the whole world sang. Happy? Of course I was happy. But why is happiness so short, so cruelly abrupt? Only a week has passed since that memorable day. Still, how different I feel. Dumb! Uninterested in life. If something doesn't happen, well—blah.

I've got to go to church this afternoon, and I know I'll never live through it. It's a cloudy-rainy day, and I feel terribly depressed. Joe has a date, Rae has a date, Daddy's playing golf, and Jack's whining. Mother's asleep. The house is so damned quiet. I think I live in an age that I don't belong in. I wish I'd lived during the Revolution when there was war! Bloodshed! And Excitement, or else when the pioneers migrated

---

97 A Portland neighborhood/district.
98 Doris's favorite aunt, Hattie Mae Bailey.

Westward and had to fight the Indians, when every day was one glorious adventure, and it was an uncertainty whether one would live 24 hours or 24 years. That was *life*!! But what is this? Just existence. Dumb, dry, lonesome existence.

I wish I was out at the O-O [ranch] now. Seated on faithful old Billy Taylor and riding across the desert. Just Marjie and I. Down that silent impenetrable canyon. Then out once more into the glad sunshine. Up, around, under. I was always contented there. There is something in the smell of sage-brush, the sight of rolling sand dunes, that makes anyone have a comfortable, happy feeling. Even the most restless person couldn't *help* but be happy on the desert. I love it! I adore it! I worship it! It is my shrine! The one object of my devotion! I live for it and it alone. Someday I'll make my home there, and never again will I have this disoriented feeling. So there!!!!!!!!!!

Later: Oh, I'm mad! mad! mad. Just before dinner this evening I was playing the Victrola and happened to look out the window, and who should I see but Gene. He motioned for me to come out, so I went. Stood on the back terrace talking to him. In a little while I glanced inside and saw that they were eating dinner, so I went in. Daddy jumped up and said, "Where have you been! We've looked all over for you!" I said I'd been out on the terrace talking to Gene, and he got so mad! Called me all sorts of names and seemed to think it was *terrible* for me to talk to a boy. And it was awful the way *he* put it. He said that I lowered myself by talking to a boy in the dark and etc. Then he ordered me out of the room. I got up and stalked out with dignity. So horrified, mad, and surprised to think of anything cutting to say. I went in the living room and could hear Daddy storming clear in there. He called me everything he could think of. Oh, these tyrannical fathers!!

Luther Raeford Bailey was a stern man and was reputed to be a "martinet," or strict disciplinarian. But Doris was Daddy's girl all her life.

Something impish inside of me made me get up, go to the piano, and play, "Nearer, My God, to Thee."[99] After I had finished there was deadly silence in the dining room. That wasn't what I wanted, so I played "Love Lifted Me."[100] He came in, of course, his face red with rage, told me not to be so damned sassy, and I was too flippant and a disgrace to the family, and blah blah. He couldn't trust me because I talked to a boy, alone in the dark, and oh! I'm so mad. I think I'll run away.

---

[99] A well-known nineteenth-century Methodist hymn, associated with the HMS *Titanic*; the band reportedly played this hymn as the ship sank.
[100] A more modern hymn, copyrighted in 1912, the year the *Titanic* went down; the hymn is about St. Peter trying to walk on water.

Monday, November 15
Decided not to run away. Too much trouble. Having an awful time with orchestra, and I wish I'd never started the damn party.

Tuesday, November 16
Nothing happened.

Wednesday, November 17
Maloney won't come if he has to bring Marjie, and everything's all mixed up, and I wish I'd never tried to give a dance. Bas[il] hasn't phoned, and I can't get an orchestra, and I almost wish I were dead.

Thursday, November 18
Well! Things are beginning to pep up and not look quite so gloomy. After school, took the Ford and went over to Alyce. Evaline can't get her car, so I wanted to talk it over with Alyce whether she would come and how. She said, "Let's run down to Jack Pillar's and ask him." So we went. Gee, I was scared because he hasn't spoken to me for two years. Anyway, he acted awfully cute and attentive. Just think, Jack Pillar, and he is cute as hell. Then I came home, and then Bill Whitely phoned and said he was coming, and every thing is hotsy totsy and I'm happy.

Friday, November 19
Well! The party went off with a bang! crash! boom! Everyone had a good time, and oh, but Jack Pillar is cute. He was nice to me, too. In fact, so nice that Alyce began to look daggers at me. And then Johnny Leverton! Cute, adorable, romantic Johnny Leverton. He dances so cute, and he's so scrumptiously romantic, tender, and fascinating. Gee! But I like him. I didn't like the way Harriet acted, tho. Awfully unrefined. Oh, say, Johnny and I were standing on the porch, and he said, "Oh, you look sweet enough

to kiss," and I said, "Why don't you?" and oh oh oh!!! I *like* him so. He has that thrilling way of speaking to you that is almost a caress. The way he says, "May I have this dance?" is enough to make any heart go *pitty pat skid skid*. Enough for Johnny. Leo was the life of the party, but I wish he wouldn't kiss me in front of Johnny—it embarrasses me. Maloney was cute as hell and by far the best looking boy there. I was proud of him. He acted so refined. The only thing wrong with the party was that three Hill boys came that weren't invited, and they were stewed to the gills. Hale and Larry were nice about getting them away. Even then we had an awful time keeping them away from Mother. When they were all leaving, Hale said, "Well, goodby, Doris" and kissed me before everyone. I was too surprised to be mad at the little devil. I like Jack Pillar and Johnny—well!!

Saturday, November 20
It rained like the devil today. I took Alyce home and stopped at a cute S.S. [Service Station]. I'm going there after this. Getting sick of Frank Heikemper [?] On the way home I passed J.L. [Johnny Leverton] and he waved. Is he cute!!! Oh my heart!! Went to Multnomah Club with Rae this evening. Tilly and Ed Mergas [were] there. I met a boy (or I guess you'd call him a man, he was 25). Rather good-looking. Fraternity man. Graduated from U. of O. Danced half the dances with him, and I'll be darned if *men* aren't worse flirts than boys.

Sunday, November 21
Slept til noon. Loafed around. Rainy day. Tired.

Monday, November 22
Ump ditty ump pa—um pa. This evening Johnny was waiting for us at the W. O.[101] line. He said "hello" to Fanny and then smiled into my eyes so

---

101 The Westover line.

that my heart began to act silly. We talked inconsequentially for a while, and then the Westover came. We started to go up on it, but Johnny said, "Oh, no, Doris, please don't go. I want to talk to you." Of course he was irresistible, so I stayed. We talked, and he got nicer and nicer. Finally, he said, "You're disappointed in me, aren't you?'

I said, "Disappointed? No, what have I got to be disappointed about?"

Then he acted kind of embarrassed and said, "Well, I have a feeling there's a little green-eyed demon flying around."

Of course I acted surprised, and I said, "Why, you silly! Why should I be jealous of you?"

And he said, "Oh, don't beat around the bush. Alyce is a cute kid, and I didn't want to kiss her, but when she hung around me like she did, there was nothing else to do but give her what she wanted, was there? But listen, Doris, I really like you lots better than her."

Well, the funny part was that I didn't know he had kissed her, tho knowing her as well as I do, I should have guessed it. Anyway, I know I was blushing, and it was nice to have him apologize to me for kissing her. It made me feel all tingly inside, and he has such pretty eyes, and I like him so. Tho of course I'll always always, always remain true to Micky, but it's nice to have little side diversions, and I hope he's down there tomorrow, but I have a feeling that he won't be.

A crowd gathers after a car wreck.

Tuesday, November 23

Of *course* Johnny wasn't down there. Darn! Bob Stryker was, tho, and he said Maloney was in the Infirmary. Boo hoo! Poor Maloney. He's a cute little devil. Harriet took her mother's Cadillac to school yesterday without permission and ran into a big Standard Oil truck. Wrecked the car all to pieces. Poor girl. I'm sorry for her. She didn't have a license, either. I WANT TO SEE JOHNNY!!

Oh say. While I was down town today *Tom Dunham* passed and *spoke to me.* I was so surprised I just said, "Oh, er, hello," and he said, "Why, hello, Doris" in a big booming voice. He's cute.

Wednesday, November 24

Johnny was on the car this morning, and he talked to me a *long* time. *Ump ditty ump pa—um pa.* He's *cute* as hell but terribly conceited. He said he'd phone me over the wk.end. This morning in Chapel they played "Moonlight and Roses."[102] Gee, but it was surprising.

---

[102] "The Andantino in D-flat," known as "Moonlight and Roses," op. 83 no. 2 for organ (1888), is one of Edwin Lemare's few well-known original compositions. American songwriters Ben Black and Charles N. Daniels added words to the melody without permission in 1921, and it became a huge hit.

Oh say. Tomorrow marks the end of the Ford. Daddy bought a Chev. Coupe, and no more will I ride in [a] rattletrap. Oh Boy!! Isn't that keen! I stopped at the cute Service Station tonight. He said, "Gee, I thought you were *never* coming back." Not so bad.

Saw Leo this afternoon. He said, "Say, was anything wrong with me Friday night? I can't remember." I shouldn't think he would. He was too drunk to even dance.

Thursday, November 25

Well, today is Thanksgiving, and I have got something to be grateful for. I said goodby to the Ford and didn't feel the least bit sorry. And the new car is so cute. Daddy let me drive the big car this afternoon. Whoopee! He said I could drive as well as the boys, too.

We had dinner at [the] Danas. Marjie's in love with Frank Lutanzi. I can't see it myself. Oh well! She probably couldn't see anything in Johnny, but *can* I? I certainly can.

Friday, November 26

Met Alyce down town, and she came home with me. We were sitting around preparing to have a dull evening when Leo and Maloney came up. Not bad—that. Leo is so sentimental, tho. About 9 o'clock Johnny L. phoned and said he was coming up. And then the fun did start. We were dancing, all alone, in the music room, and he kissed me. Oh! I've never had a kiss like that before. It was WONDERFUL. My knees felt all shaky, and I felt all tingly inside. He kissed me once, twice, three times and so on. Oh! And each one was better than the one before. Gee, oh gosh, oh gee! I'm in love! After that he would hold my hand and do little things that would send the blood pounding in my face. Oh, I like him so.

Maloney isn't half bad either. Gee! but we had a good time. And Johnny *does* kiss so nicely. Much nicer than Leo or Maloney and *almost* as nice as Moody.

Saturday, November 27

Slept late. Johnny came up and took us to the game. Alyce managed to hang onto him. She was even so desperate that she wouldn't let him sit next to me. Oh well! I had a good time anyway. Saw Jack Freidel and Jack Pillar, two old flames. I don't see how I ever could have liked Jack Freidel. He's dumb-looking. Jack Pillar is adorable, tho. Leo called up this evening, but I couldn't have him come up because the folks were going out. Damn. Wrote a book report. Sleepy!!

Sunday, November 28

Mother let me drive the new car to church. Fun! Went for a ride this afternoon to see somebody's new baby. Mother made a big fuss about it and raved about how *beautiful* it was. It looked just like any other baby to me except it had a big upper lip. I've decided I don't like Johnny any more, or Moody, or Leo or Maloney or Bas. or any of them. They're shallow, conceited, mercenary, disgusting, two-faced, cheap, obnoxious, fickle, and I hate them. I don't know a single boy that is worthwhile. So I'm going to swear off of them. I'm not even going to look at a good-looking man. *I HATE MEN!!!! Oh*, they're awful. I'm going to put my mind on studying and ignore the whole damn bunch.

Monday, November 29

Uninteresting day. Took car for a while this afternoon. I'm still sworn off of men even if life isn't *quite* as interesting. I'll show them that we girls aren't as dependent on them as they think we are. Their conceit is more than I can stand.

Tuesday, November 30

"Ashes to ashes, dust to dust." Another woman was strangled today.[103] I wish I was a detective. I'll bet I could find the murderer. Also—Opal Barnes, the maid we had before this one, was taken to the Pen[itentiary] for stealing $3,000 worth of clothes, money, and jewelry. I always thought there was something fishy about her. Her husband's in the jail at Tacoma for white slavery, too. Hot dog! She's going to the bad; that just shows where men lead you to. It was by a man that that woman was strangled and by a man that Opal was led astray. It just goes to show that "You can't trust men." Oh, how I hate them!![104]

Wednesday, December 1

A rotten day. Both in weather, atmosphere, disposition, and etc. It might snow if it doesn't rain—alas! Who knows? I feel dumb tonight, so I guess I [won't] write any thing. My vocabulary might run away with me.

Thursday, December 2

Met "Nemerosky" on the street car, and he rode up with me. He's cute for a Jew.[105] Had car for a while and went to Service Station. Mac acted awfully attentive. Alyce phoned and raved about Jack P. and John L. I wasn't even jealous because I'm through with the masculine gender. Enough is enough, says I.

---

103 Earl Leonard Nelson, aka "The Dark Strangler" and "The Gorilla Murderer," killed twenty-two women during this time period in the San Francisco Bay Area; Nelson was killing in Portland in November 1926. He eventually continued his spree back East and into Canada.

104 She is using the language of the Women's Temperance Union (largely responsible for Prohibition) here and sounds like a reformer.

105 Dating outside of her religion would have been strictly forbidden.

Friday, December 3

Stayed home from school with [a] cold. Took the car this afternoon. Saw Basil Brown and took him down town. He told me all his family troubles and etc. He's going with Dorothy Rogers now. Says he likes her better than Frances. I can't see it myself. After that, saw Laurance Moody. He didn't see me, but my heart went *pity pat skid skid* as I gazed upon his golden hair. He is so good looking. Not the type I'd want to marry, tho.

I'd want my husband to be tall, slim, and dark. Blue eyes, the kind that twinkled when he laughed and turned black when he was mad. A straight Aquiline nose and a boyish laughing mouth. A firm chin with just loads of character, and I'd want his whole appearance to be jaunty, carefree, Debonaire, and Romantic. He'd have to be able to make love furiously but not seriously. I wouldn't want him to be serious. Ever. Even if he was facing a danger. I'd want him to be the kind that laughs in death's face. I HATE SERIOUS PEOPLE. Oh, yes, he'd be adventuresome. Ready to do and dare and accept the consequences. That would be an ideal husband.

—Alas! I'm afraid no such man lives, so of course I'll never get married. I'd only marry this type.

After I had written this, John, June, and Chauncy came up. We were outside talking, and Seth Burroughs came out of Catlin's[106] and came over. Seth is cute—in a way. They stayed about an hour.

Saturday, December 4

Went to foot ball game this afternoon—exciting. Saw Volmar Van Horn. He doesn't look nearly as romantic as he is. I hadn't seen him since last June. Also saw Margie S., Lorraine, Perry, and a bunch of others. Basil and Dorothy Rogers included. Those two are becoming inseparable. We saw

---

106 Ruth Catlin began Miss Catlin's School in 1911 on Lovejoy Avenue, moving into the school building she had constructed on Culpepper Terrace (the street where Doris lived) in 1917. This later became the Catlin Gabel School, still extant today.

Johnny this evening, and he's too conceited to talk to, or about. Went to a show tonight. Good! Dull life! I want my Micky!!!!!!!!!!!!

Sunday, December 5
Went to church and sat close to a good-looking man. Gene came over this afternoon. He's as conceited as ever. This evening Joe and I took the car and went to C.E. [Christian Endeavor]. Afterward I took Joe to Bob's, and I went to Alyce's. We went for a ride and decided to go to Jack Pillar's and show him the new car. So we did. Took him for a ride. And was he nice! Oh boy! He said how sorry he was that I lived so far away and asked me to come oftener and was—oh! Awfully nice. Gave me all kinds of cute little compliments and let it be known—generally that he didn't hate me. Everything is hotsy totsy now!!!

Monday, December 6
School's dumb as ever. I saw Leo, Johnny, and Bob Stryker this afternoon. Bob's been in a big fight and has a broken nose. Poor kid.

Tuesday, December 7
Alyce is having Johnny and Jack over next Sunday, and she invited me. Hot diggity! I'm crazy about Jack.

Wednesday, December 8
Dull day.

Thursday, December 9
Johnny sat with us on the street car this morning. He's terribly unsophisticated. Blah!! Saw my Secret Sorrow[107] on the car. I can't wait until Sunday. Then I'll see Jack.

---

107 Perhaps she means Frank Norris from September 20.

184

Friday, December 10

Rather uninteresting day. Maloney waved to me from automobile. Johnny phoned to see if I was going to Alyce's Sunday. Bob and Chauncey came up. I had just washed my hair, and it was straight. Oh well. I didn't care about them. Going Xmas shopping tomorrow.

Saturday, December 11

I got my hair curled and went Xmas shopping. I'm broke now, but I'm glad it's over with. This afternoon the phone rang, and a deep masculine voice said, "This is Santa Claus!" Of course I knew it wasn't, but I kidded him along, and it turned out to be Jack Pillar. He asked me if I was going to Alyce's tomorrow, and I said—I don't think so—just to see what he would say. He said, "Well! If you're not going, neither am I!" Isn't that nice? We talked for nearly half hour and it only seemed like 10 minutes, and he's so darn cute. I'm looking forward to tomorrow with a great deal of anticipation. If something exciting doesn't happen, it won't be my fault.

Marjie D. went to [the] Hill dance tonight. Lucky! I wish we were on the same party list.

Sunday, December 12

This afternoon Joe and I took the car and went by for Johnny. I took the boys to Alyce's and went down to call for Jack. After that we played cards. Then took the car and went to see Bee. She's married and living in a perfectly cute stucco cottage. The boys got restless, so we took Joe to Lorraine's and the four of us went for a ride. Yes! Jack kissed me. After waiting two whole years, he kissed me and oh boy! I've been missing something.

We drove for ages, having a perfectly scrumptious time, and then I let Jack drive. About 7 o'clock it began to snow. And it snowed and snowed and snowed. The windshield wipers froze, and Jack had to stick his cute curly head out in the cold to see to drive. The road was terribly slippery, but we finally got back to Alyce's about 9 o'clock. We had something to eat and then sat by the fire, and Jack sang romantic songs. I'll never forget that blissful hour. Then Jack suggested that we drive by for Joe, so we did. Only we didn't go straight there. We drove around for a long time, and Jack became Romantic, serious, and thrilling. We discussed life, convention, and necking. Everything considered, we had a hell of a good time. Then we got Joe and Johnny and headed for home. Left Jack at his house and proceeded on our way.

Of course I had a good time the rest of the way, since Johnny was beside me. But by that time the snow was a foot deep on the hill, and after we left Johnny, it took us an hour to climb it. Then we burnt out a berring [*sic*] and had to leave the car halfway up the hill. Of course the folks were mad as hell, and Joe told them that Jack and I went for a ride. Now I can't have the car for two months and a date either. The speedometer registered 90 miles, and of course that made them sore. Oh well! Such is life and it was worth it. I'm happy and it was worth it. I'll never forget the way he kisses. Tenderly, masterfully, thrillingly. Gee! but he's cute.

It does not always snow in Portland in the winter, but when it does, the young people get out and enjoy it. Rae and Joe Bailey play outside the house with their dog, Fritz the Spitz, circa 1914.

Monday, December 13

Oh! Oh! Oh! Oh! *Oh.* This evening the folks went out, and about 7:30 Gene came over and asked me to go sleighing with him. Since there wasn't anything else to do, I went. We went down to Reyleh hill,[108] watching a big toboggan being pulled up the hill. When it got to the top, one of the boys said, "Hello, Doris." Then some other voice said, "Is that Doris Bailey?" and the first voice said "yes," and the other one said, "Ye gods, I know that woman," and came over behind me. It was too dark to see him until he got close, and he said, "Well, hello, Doris, aren't you going to welcome me back?"

I looked up, expecting to see some Lincoln hick, but what I saw sent my heart to my feet, then to my head, then pounding madly. What I saw was about 5 ft. 8 [inches] of tall, black-haired handsomeness dressed in a sailor suit. It was Jack Hibbard. Jack, who I hadn't seen since last June. Oh dear diary, *you* know how I felt. I just stared at him and tried to talk.

When I did find my voice, the words came fast and furious. Before I realized it, we were pulled on the toboggan, 20 of us, and shouting down the hill, Jack's protective arm about me. Three times we went up and down, and I was in a haven of blissfulness. Even the fact that Moody and Larry and Basil and Bill were all around me didn't seem to make any impression on me.

I forgot that I once thought I loved Moody and had been madly in love with Larry. I forgot everything but the fact that Jack was near me. Talking, laughing, flashing his boyish smile and talking in his sweet, adorable voice. About 10 o'clock we began to feel cold, so Bill, Jack, [Bobby] L'doo, and a couple of girls came up to our house to get warm. We made hot coffee and danced and talked. Jack told us all about the Navy, and then somehow or other, Jack and I were alone.

---

108 Raleigh Hills neighborhood, west Portland.

He looked at me and said, "At last!" Strode over to me. Took me in his arms and kissed me as I've never been kissed before. A real kiss. Not just a playful peck. He leaned me way back and pressed his burning lips on mine. I felt weak when he let go of me. And he is so handsome. If I live for a hundred years, I'll never forget that kiss. Never, never, never. It was real, alive, burning with passion and feeling. I know I don't love him, but I feel all jumpy when I think about him. It is now after one, but I'm not the least bit sleepy.

Tuesday, December 14

It was cold today. Down to 19 degrees. Of course I couldn't keep my mind off of Jack H. He is so utterly different from what he used to be. When I first knew him last fall, he was boyish, unaffected, inclined to seriousness, trustful, adorable, and innocent. Now he has a certain hardness about him. He laughs just as often, but it's so affected. The way he talks, dances, looks and laughs, yes, and even loves, tho I can't say I object to that. He has such an obvious layer of sophistication over his sweet adorable self. He hides himself behind a wall of reserve and doesn't let his true nature come to light. He's seeing life in the raw, and he isn't the type that can stand it. People that didn't know him would say he was too damn cock-sure of himself. Too jaunty and arrogant. Too much conceit combined with toughness, but I know that underneath he must be the same boyish Jack that I knew.

Wednesday, December 15

Stayed home from school because the street cars weren't running. This evening Jack Hibbard phoned and asked me if I was going sleighing. Was I! Joe and Gene took me down, but it was cold and they wouldn't stay, so I had to come home without seeing him. I was moping around the house, and the phone rang. I expected it to be Jack, but it was Bob Ziegler. We talked a while and then hung up. About 9 o'clock [in the evening] the phone rang again, and it was Jack. He told me to meet him behind the garage at 9:20, which I did. Then we went *in* the garage where it was warm, and talked and talked. He wouldn't come in the house because he thought it was too late. But we stayed out there ages, that is, until Mother began to miss me. Then we had a WONDERFUL goodby kiss. Oh my poor little heart! It can't stand much more of this. He was much more natural this evening, too. More like his own sweet adorable self.

~~He gave me a piece of gum[?] that I'm going to keep forever.~~

Thursday, December 16

I saw Johnny Leverton on the car this morning, and he stopped and talked to me. He's cute. This evening we went to the Pantages[109] and saw Babe Ruth. He's not so much to rave about. Terribly conceited.

Friday, December 17

This morning on the street car a good looking boy sat across from us. He looked terribly familiar, so I pointed him out to Fanny. She nearly went into hysterics and said, "Why, don't you remember, that's the boy that chased us last summer in a car on Willamette Heights, and we talked to him and told him we [were] from U. of O., and he made a date with us!" Of course I remembered. Only he was twice as good looking as before. He has the most marvelous blue eyes and mustache. I was too embarrassed, tho, to recognize him. Every time I looked up, I could feel his eyes on me. Gee! He's cute.

Went to Harriet Avery's tonight. Larry was there, and so was Bobby L'Doo. Also two other hicks. We had a pretty good time. Just so-so. They were the kind of boys that know nothing but to neck, drink, and be dumb. One boy was especially disgusting. He'd stick his big nose down on my face, and the liquor on his breath was terrible. Ugh! I hate to think about it. Larry was sweet, tho, and so was Bobby. But none of them compare with Jack.

---

[109] Pantages Theater, at Broadway and Alder Street. She saw Babe Ruth live onstage.

Saturday, December 18

Did some Xmas shopping this morning and then went to Alyce's. We went to a show in the evening. After the show we were feeling extra devilish, so we rang the bell of an apt. house, asked for Mr. Payne, talked Babytalk to him, and told him we would be right up. Then we went home and called up Jack Pillar's cousin and asked to speak to Santa Claus. I talked to him a long time, kidded him along. About 1 o'clock [in the morning] we called up everyone we could think of just to get them out of bed. Silly, weren't we? Oh well!

Sunday, December 19

Came home this morning. Went to [the] Danas in the afternoon. Saw Ned Gervais. He's not as cute as he used to be. Dull life.

Monday, December 20

Whole family's sick. Mother, Joe, Rae, Jack. Hell of a life. Bummed around the house all day. This time last Monday—oh boy. Jack was giving me one of those affected sophisticated sailor kisses. Hot diggity. Opportunity comes once in a lifetime. Why didn't I [grab] it and run away with him? Elope? I know—because he didn't ask me to.

Tuesday, December 21

Well! Well! Well! Guess Joe has Scarlet Fever. If we all have to be quarantined, I'll die! That's all. I got my Xmas present today—a sweet adorable fluffy Pekingese Spitz! She's a little Thoroughbred. Gee, but I'm crazy about her. Full of pep and a perfect little beauty. Name's Patsy.

Wednesday, December 22

Made candy and bummed around. Had car this afternoon and went over to Grant. Incidentally saw Jack. He had dislocated his knee since I saw him last. It's funny. The last time I saw him, I was crazy about him, and this time he didn't even stir my heart. He has a funny shaped mouth, and his ears are too big. He's a nut. I don't like him. That last Sunday I would have been willing to go to the end of the world with him. Today I wouldn't go to a dog-fight with him. That's why I'm never going to get married. Opinions change too quickly.

Thursday, December 23

Washed dog and my hair. Got a marcel and went over to Alyce's. That's all. Dull life. Joe has Scarlet fever. They didn't quarantine us, but no one can come to the house.

Friday, December 24

Xmas Eve! Exactly a year ago, a small boy, exuberant at the thought of the morrow, ran heedlessly across a street, was struck by an auto and instantly killed. Oh, the joys and sorrows that everyone has suffered in a year!

Jack Pillar sent me a Christmas card! He signed it *(golddigger) Jack*. Gee! But he took our teasing seriously. He's a cute little mutt, but I don't like him. Like my dog lots better. Of course he isn't romantic like Jack, but then—Jack isn't soft and fluffy like the dog. So that's that.

Saturday, December 25

Xmas Day!!! I got the usual amount of silk stockings, silk underwear, handkerchiefs, powder puff, plus an adorable set of bookends for my room, a ring, a bracelet, couple of dresser sets, scarf, antimacassar[110] and etc. A merry time was had by all. Forgot to say Daddy gave me an adorable pair of silk pajamas. Cute!!

---

110 A small cloth or doily placed over the backs or arms of chairs or sofas to protect the furniture from being stained.

191

I decided this evening that I'm going to let Love come to me. When a good looking suitor appears, I'm going to act natural, and he can take me or leave me. None of this "holding on" business for me. Love is going to come in a flurry of gladness. There isn't going to be anything cold and calculating about it. Just Romance, and beauty, and happiness. I want to give, give, give to the man I love. And I want to love him with my very soul. So that my heart sings and dances at his very presence.

Sunday, December 26
Dumb, dumb day. Monotonous life.

Tuesday, December 28
Met Marjie down town, and we went to lunch and bummed around. Then we came out to her house in the Chev. And she had some kids down for the evening. Good time and all that sort of thing. Tomorrow morning we're driving in early, and I'm going to have my nose operated on.[111]

Friday, December 31
New Year's Eve! I'm sick as a dog. Came home this morning, and while my nose was still being bandaged, the Doctor discovered that I had Scarlet Fever. As if my nose isn't enough trouble without that. Damn it all to hell. Probably have to go to the Isolation Hospital for a month and miss all that school!!

---

111 Perhaps because of the accident with the iron bar in the gym some months before.

List of - well, - ahem, ! What would you call
them? Infatuations?

1. Bruce Cambell - blue eyes
2. Bob Ziegler - brown eyes
3. Perry - grey eyes (blah! how could I ?)
—4 ~~Jack Peter~~ brown eyes
5. Hal Paddock - blue eyes
6. Lloyd Buchanan - " "
7. Fredrich (Fridgi) - marvelous grey eyes
=8 Jack Preickel (the dalmeat last) Blue eyes
=9 ~~Grayson~~ Shinns (Micky) (I love him) Blue eyes
=10. Jack Hibbard (oh he's wonderful !!) Blue
11. ~~Bob Hibbard (simply scruptuous) Blue~~
12 Volmor Van Horn (cute !!!) Blue eyes
13 Buddy Powell (blue eyes, fast !!)
~~14 ed Bat~~
14. Fritzi (another Fritzi !) wonderful dancer
15 Jess Pennington (an adorable cowboy)
                                    brown eyes

After the 1925–1926 Diaries

There is more to come in the Doris Diaries. Doris went into the isolation ward in January 1927 for scarlet fever, and there she contracted diphtheria and almost died. She came out in early March 1927 and stayed out of school to rest. She fell ill again in the fall, however, when her appendix burst, and upon her recovery, her family moved to Los Angeles for a few weeks and then to the Arizona desert for her convalescence. Doris stayed in Arizona for several months, eventually returning to Portland and St. Helen's Hall to finish high school.

Her Arizona desert adventures included racing horses, bucking broncos (after an appendix operation!), and romances with cowboys and later, from afar, her Portland doctor. And her beloved, dissipated Micky came back into the picture.

Further adventures awaited as Doris entered college in both Arizona and Portland through the Great Depression. Later, World War II loomed on the horizon, and Doris headed to San Francisco and to true love at last. The war diaries are not to be missed; through them, we witness Doris become political and hone her writing craft to a keen edge.

Stay tuned for more Doris adventures online via Twitter (twitter/thedorisdiaries) and Facebook (facebook.com/thedorisdiaries) as well the website (www.thedorisdiaries.com).

Where Did She Go?

Where did she go, the girl long-legged

with slim pretty ankles, so sure of her step

so sure of her future,

so proud of her stature?

Now in her place is this aged lady,

whose ankles are thick and whose step

is not steady.

Her eyes not so bright, her smile not so ready.

Was she always there biding her time

until she was ready to emerge from the girl

and to taunt the vain one

whose life was so heady?

Or is the girl even now inside the lady

waiting the day until she is free

to escape the aged body and walk once again —

proud of her legs that dance on the lea?

Doris Bailey Murphy, June 2000

Appendix I:
Glossary of Doris's Slang

Back number: literally, an out-of-date issue of a magazine; old-fashioned

Big egg: a person who lives the big life, high-class

Blooie: when everything goes to pieces, an explosion

Bosh: absurd talk, nonsense

Bummed (around): stayed in, at home; lazy

Bunk: nonsense

Cheap: of little account or value, shoddy, embarrassed, sheepish

Chum/chummy: close friend or companion; friendly, intimate, sociable

Collegiate: characteristic of college students, neat and proper

Common: vulgar, cheap, inferior

Course: class schedule

Cut: to ignore or avoid socially

Cut up: act silly

Dago: A dark-skinned person of Hispanic or Italian heritage; a racial slur

Egg: see **Big egg**

Gay: happy, lighthearted

Hammer: hang around, spend time

High hat: snobbish, haughty

Hot dog!: exclamation of joy. Also **Hot diggity!**

Hotsy-totsy: pleasing, wonderful

In dutch: in trouble; could also mean pregnant

Keen: fantastic, wonderful fun

Kerflunk: a sudden muffled thud or sound, like an explosion or flat tire; ruined or wasted

Knickers: loose-fitting short trousers gathered at the knee; a style for men, sometimes worn for golf; girls wore them for riding horses or under a dress.

Knows his onions: knows his business

Line: patter or way of speaking

Make love to: to pitch woo, to engage in amorous speech and caressing

Marcel: to put waves/curls in the hair, a woman's hairstyle (named for the inventor of the Marcel curling iron)

Mugging: kissing

Mutt: inept, ignorant, or stupid person

Necking: passionate kissing

Peach: a person or thing that is especially attractive, liked, or enjoyed

Peck: a large quantity, a lot; technically, eight dry quarts measurement

Pep/Peppy: energy or high spirits

Petting: heavier necking, "feeling up"

Program: her dance card; a printed, numbered card with blank lines on which to write the names of boys who asked her to dance. A girl could keep track of which dance was available or engaged, and keep the program for a souvenir.

Sheik: a man with sex appeal, a boyfriend

Snappy: smart, lively, slick

Snub: to rudely avoid. See **Cut**

Soaked: drunk

Spiffy: an elegant appearance, nice

Stewed: drunk

Swell: wonderful

Rave: enthuse, talk excitedly

Rushing: Pursuing enthusiastically.

Take the cake: to surpass all others, either positively or negatively; extraordinary or unusual. From the carnival game of Cake Walk, where the winner literally takes (wins) a cake.

Take (him/her) to a dog fight, wouldn't: wouldn't spend even the least bit of time or money with such an unworthy person

Tall language: profanity

Thick: stupid, slow, or insensitive; also **Chummy**

Tough: wild, unchaperoned (a party); uncivilized, of a lower social class (a person)

Uppish: arrogant, condescending, uppity

Vamp/vamping: to use feminine charms on, flirt

Appendix II:
Pop Culture

Movies

Beverly of Graustark: *Beverly of Graustark* (1926) is a silent film starring Marion Davies, Creighton Hale, and Antonio Moreno. Beverly Calhoun impersonates the Prince of Graustark to claim his birthright while he recovers from an accident and, in the meantime, falls for the prince's bodyguard.

The Arab: Most likely Doris saw *The Arab* (1924), by MGM/Samuel Goldwyn, filmed in Algiers with native Bedouins as extras.

For Heaven's Sake: In *For Heaven's Sake* (1926), the Uptown Boy, played by Harold Lloyd, is a millionaire playboy who falls for the Downtown Girl, played by Jobyna Ralston, who works in Brother Paul's mission. Hilarity ensues.

Pathe News: Pathé Newsreels were produced from 1910 until the 1970s, when production of newsreels in general stopped due to television's universality. Newsreels were shown in the cinema, and in the early days they were silent; they ran for about four minutes and were issued biweekly.

Stella Dallas: This is a 1925 silent film produced by Sam Goldwyn/MGM Studios. The film stars Douglas Fairbanks Jr., among others.

Celebrities

Jack Dempsey: Professional boxer who held the World Heavyweight Championship from 1919 to 1926. Dempsey was one of the most popular boxers in history. Many of his fights set financial and attendance records, including the first million-dollar gate.

Harold Lloyd: Harold Lloyd was one of the most popular and influential film comedians of the silent film era. Lloyd made nearly 200 comedy films, both silent and "talkies," between 1914 and 1947. His movies often featured extended chase scenes and daredevil tricks.

Babe Ruth: George Herman Ruth Jr., best known as Babe Ruth, was an American baseball player who spent twenty-two seasons (1914–1935) in Major League Baseball playing for three teams: the Boston Red Sox, the New York Yankees, and the Boston Braves. During the 1920s, Ruth toured major cities talking about his career as a Yankee, often accompanied by a short film depicting "The House That Ruth Built" (i.e., Yankee Stadium). In the fall of 1926 the Pantages Theaters paid Ruth $100,000 to do a twelve-week, in-person tour of their theaters. He was a one-man show, jumping through a tissue-paper hoop at the start of each performance. A handwritten letter that Ruth wrote on Pantages Theater, Portland, stationery is dated December 16, 1926, the day before Doris saw him.

Rudolph Valentino: Rudolph Valentino was a sex symbol of the 1920s, known as the "Latin Lover." He starred in several well-known silent films, including *The Sheik*, *Blood and Sand*, and *Son of the Sheik*. The 1920s slang word for boyfriend or sexy man, *sheik*, comes from Valentino's film roles.

Portland Theaters

Broadway Theatre: Originally located at 1008 Broadway. The Broadway Theatre opened in 1926 and operated into the 1980s, but was demolished in 1988.

"The Helie": The Heilig Theatre was located at Broadway and Taylor Street. In 1929 Paramount Pictures took over and renamed the place The Rialto. It was renamed the Mayfair Theatre in the 1930s; the venue also operated as the Music Box during its lifetime. The theater building was demolished in 1997.

Hollywood Theatre: The Hollywood Theatre is a central historical point of the Hollywood District in northeast Portland. It was built in 1926 at 4122 Sandy Boulevard. (Note: Portland addresses changed in 1933, so this may not be the original address.)

The Music Box Theatre: The Music Box was a popular name for theaters in Portland; one source says there were as many as six theaters with that name over time. The one Doris likely attended was on Alder Street. It opened in 1911 as the People's Theater and was renamed the Music Box and then the Alder Theatre. It had a 2/9 Wurlitzer organ.

The Nob Hill: Located at Kearny Street at 23rd Avenue, the Nob Hill Theatre was a small neighborhood theater that opened in 1912. It was renamed the Esquire Theatre in 1938. The Esquire Theatre closed in 1987, when the theater auditorium and box office were demolished. The remaining space was converted to a retail space.

The Pantages Theatre: There was a Pantages Family Theatre in Portland in 1915; it offered live shows, vaudeville performances, and even circus acts. In the 1920s it began to show silent films. The Pantages Theatre was located at Broadway and Alder Street.

Other Entertainment

The Oasis: The Crystal Springs Oasis was a tea room on Sandy Boulevard at 162nd Avenue, known then as Barker Road. There was also a restaurant called The Oasis on SW Yamhill, about where Pioneer Place/Saks is today. Doris could be referring to either but probably meant the former, since she said she would "go out to the Oasis." Live music and entertainment along with illicit booze were suggested.

The Student Prince: *The Student Prince* is an operetta in four acts with music by Sigmund Romberg. It opened December 2, 1924, on Broadway in New York. Doris saw it with her brother Rae in May 1926 in Portland.

Zane Grey: An American author of adventure stories that take place in the Wild West. *Riders of the Purple Sage* (1912) was his best-known work. Grey was a major force in shaping the myths of the Old West, in Hollywood and in the popular imagination.

Photo Credits

Rae Bailey, a lifelong shutterbug, and his beloved Kodak box camera, circa 1918. He took most of the photos in this book; they were preserved in a photo album for eighty or more years. Most of the photos were smaller than two inches square and their details never seen until newly scanned and enlarged for this book.

Page

1   Doris Louise Bailey, studio portrait, circa 1927, Portland, Oregon. Courtesy of the Bailey family.

6   Bailey Family, studio portrait, 1908, Cambridge, Massachusetts. Courtesy of the Bailey family.

11   Diary 1. Photo by Julia Park Tracey.

Cover photos: Doris, age twelve, studio portrait; Luther R. Bailey, Doris, and Joe in car at 1320 Alameda Avenue; Rae's friend Mary Rawlings wringing out her bathing suit. All photos courtesy of the Bailey family. Cover design by Eric J. Kos.

Author photo, Julia Park Tracey, by J. Astra Brinkman, copyright 2012.

Selected Bibliography

Allen, Frederick Lewis. *Only Yesterday—An Informal History of the Nineteen Twenties*. New York: Harper and Row, 1957.

Architectural Heritage Center. http://www.visitahc.org. May 14, 2012

Blackman, Cally. *20th Century Fashion: The 20s and 30s; Flappers and Vamps*. Milwaukee: Gareth Stevens Publishing, 2000.

Blocksma, Mary. *Ticket to the Twenties*. Boston: Little, Brown, 1993.

Boardman, Barrington. *Flappers, Bootleggers, Typhoid Mary and the Bomb: An Anecdotal History of the United States from 1923-1945*. New York: Harper and Row, 1989.

Cinema Treasures. http://www.cinematreasures.org. May 13, 2012

Corrigan, Jim. *The 1920s Decade in Photos: The Roaring Twenties*. Berkeley Heights, NJ: Enslow, 2010.

Crimezzz. http://www.crimezz.net. March 12, 2012

Del Mar, David Peterson. *Oregon's Promise*. Corvallis: Oregon State University Press, 2003.

Dietrich, William. *Northwest Passage: The Great Columbia River*. Seattle: University of Washington Press, 2003.

Dodds, Gordon B. *Oregon: A History.* New York: Norton, 1977.

Fitzgerald, Kimberli. "Rice MPS and Gregg House Nomination." http://www.kimfitzgerald.net. Sept. 20, 2011

"Inflation Calculator." *DaveManuel.com.* http://www.davemanuel.com/inflation-calculator.php. March 12, 2012.

"Love Lifted Me." *Hymn Studies,* Sept. 15, 2008. http://homeschoolblogger.com/hymnstudies/. May 13, 2012

"The Marcel Wave." *1920-30.com.* http://www.1920-30.com/fashion/hairstyles/marcel-wave.html. April 27, 2012

McCartney, Laton. *Across the Great Divide: Robert Stuart and the Discovery of the Oregon Trail.* New York: Free Press, 2003.

Murphy, Doris B. *Love and Labor.* New York: iUniverse, 2006.

National Archives. Fourteenth Census of the United States, 1920. Records of the Bureau of the Census.

Noggle, Burl. *Into the Twenties: The United States from Armistice to Normalcy.* Urbana: University of Illinois Press, 1974.

"Old Portland Street Names." Scribd. http://www.scribd.com/doc/55766497/Old-Portland-Street-Names. April 20, 2012.

The Oregon Encyclopedia. http://www.oregonencyclopedia.org. April 20, 2012.

Oregon Historical Society. http://www.ohs.org. April 20, 2012.

Oregon State Board of Health. *Biennial Report,* 1910–1926. University of California Berkeley Library.

PDX History. http://www.pdxhistory.com. April 20, 2012.

Poekel, Charlie. *Babe and the Kid: The Legendary Story of Babe Ruth and Johnny Sylvester*. Charleston, SC: History Press, 2007.

Reser, Harry, and his Orchestra, with Tom Stacks (vocals). "I've Got Some Lovin' to Do." Recorded 1926 by The Six Hayseeds, New York, Vocalion.

Rupp, Leila J. "Feminism and the Sexual Revolution in the Early Twentieth Century: The Case of Doris Stevens." *Feminist Studies* 15.2 (Summer 1989).

"Silent Era Theaters." *Silent Era*. http://www.silentera.com/theaters/USA/ oregon/portland/. April 15, 2012.

Wilde, Oscar. *The Importance of Being Earnest*. The Pennsylvania State University, Pennsylvania. 2009.

Wright, Gladys. "Salute to Billie Bailey." *Upshaw Family Journal* (July 1977).

Index

CPSIA information can be obtained at www.ICGtesting.com
Printed in the USA
LVOW101144081012

301959LV00001B/9/P